*This is a book on religion (in complete
accord with the <u>Scriptures</u>) which never
once resorts to mystical, magical or
supernatural explanations of anything;
and which attacks, with complete candor,
the most <u>baffling</u> concepts of religious
doctrine, <u>stripping</u> them once and for
all of their <u>aura</u> of mystery.*

IS GOD SUPERNATURAL?
The 4,000-Year Misunderstanding

An Exegesis by R. L. Dione
Author of *God Drives a Flying Saucer*

Bantam Books, by R. L. Dione

GOD DRIVES A FLYING SAUCER
IS GOD SUPERNATURAL? THE
4,000-YEAR MISUNDERSTANDING

IS
GOD
SUPERNATURAL?

*The 4,000-Year
Misunderstanding*

An Exegesis* by
R. L. DIONE

---

* An exegesis is a critical interpretation of a text,
particularly a portion of Scripture.

IS GOD SUPERNATURAL?
A Bantam Book / May 1976

Published simultaneously in the United States and Canada

Bantam Books are published by Bantam Books, Inc. Its trade-
mark, consisting of the words "Bantam Books" and the
portrayal of a bantam, is registered in the United States
Patent Office and in other countries. Marca Registrada. Bantam
Books, Inc., 666 Fifth Avenue, New York, New York 10019.

PRINTED IN THE UNITED STATES OF AMERICA

To my children, Robert, Stevan, Donald, Michelle, and Janine, and to all the children of the world, I dedicate this book with the promise that the coming age of reason will find the society of man more mature and more humane.

Acknowledgments

Down through the ages of history great men of science have been persecuted for advocating views contrary to popular subscription. Galileo, Pasteur and Newton should therefore serve as <u>sentinels</u> to warn us that popularity is not a prerequisite for truth. Each of these great men suffered persecution and ridicule at the hands of their contemporaries, but each of them emerged victorious on the battlefield of ideas.

Now working independently on his farm in Bedminster, Penn., Bruce DePalma, a former M.I.T. instructor, has barely begun his battle to gain acceptance for his excitingly new anti gravity theories. But I am confident that, when the smoke clears away, this brilliant physicist will stand shoulder to shoulder with the great scientists of all ages.

I extend to him and his associates my deep appreciation for permission to use the experiments appearing in the appendix.

R. L. Dione

Author's Note

The Bible quotations and spellings in this book were taken from the Douay-Challoner Old Testament and from the Confraternity New Testament and Psalms. These translations comprise the standard Catholic Bible which differs in many respects from the King James Protestant Bible.

The Protestant Bible omits seven books of the Old Testament as well as parts of two others. It changes names and spellings and sometimes changes wording. The Apocalypse, the last book of the New Testament, is called Revelations in the King James Bible. The King James' Noah is Noe in the standard Catholic, and the King James' Joshua is Josue in the standard Catholic.

In the following text, all quotations from the standard Catholic version which do not appear in the King James version are noted by asterisk as being a Book from The Apocrypha.

Contents

Introduction

The belief that life has meaning and is not the result of a spectacular series of accidents of nature is, and always has been, the driving force behind man's belief in a supreme being. To think that we are born, struggle, love, fight, and finally die for no other reason than to satisfy the conditions of some grotesque sequence of accidental events is more than man has ever been able to accept. As a consequence, every culture on earth has a religion.

The tremendous variety of these religions would seem to preclude the possiblity that they all are inspired by the same god. The problem then becomes: Are all these religions the result of fantasy? Or is there perhaps only one faith which is inspired by God, leaving all the rest only the imaginative creations of their originators?

If indeed there is a supreme being, it would seem absurd to suggest that He'd not see to it that all His children had at least the chance to know His rules for living and thus have an equal chance for salvation.

And, since I am convinced of the existence of God, I propose that those who "nitpick" the Bible waste their time; that God, in His wisdom, has given to man (through all the great religions) rules for right living, and that the common denominator threading through the eleven great religions of the world is the plea for mankind to treat his neighbor with consideration. To think, for example, that it makes a difference to God whether or not we are dunked in or splashed with water at baptism is to accord to God no more intelligence than we might expect of an imbecile. And, we might

1

add, to expect man in this day and age to believe in a supernatural god is equally absurd. But, to those who would hold in contempt the ritual and ceremony of formal religions (seeing in these activities evidence of intellectual stagnation and outright ignorance), it should be pointed out that any act focusing attention on God promotes ethical behavior. And this would be the case whether or not God is real.

The proud intellectual who in the past considered himself above such things as submission to a belief in God will find in these pages proof that man is not an accident of nature and that he therefore owes his existence to a creator. He will find that this Creator, God, is physical and, as the Bible teaches, eternal. He will learn why God created him, and he will learn what God has planned for his future. And, finally, in these pages will be found the answers to many of the mysteries involving the technology alluded to but never explained in the Scriptures. In sum, this book is directed at the atheist or skeptic whose common sense demands something more than allegories, superstition, and blind faith to convince him that the Scriptures do indeed describe a supreme creator.

But the most amazing fact of all is that the conversion of the atheist, promised here, will be accomplished without the slightest deviation from the teachings of the Bible. For it will be shown that a colossal misinterpretation of the greatest religious book ever written is responsible for the recent exodus of reasonable people from the realm of the believers.

It should take nothing more than common sense to convince anyone of the validity of the ethics taught in the Great Book, but because certain elements of the Bible seem to contradict reason, there are those who conclude that the Scriptures are nothing more than the imaginative creations of ancient scribes and thus deserve no more respect than the myths and folklore of various peoples of the past.

To add to the consternation of the general public, we have, today, experts in theology and biblical interpretation who propose diametrically opposed views of the meanings of various passages of Scripture, and we have historians and linguistics experts who have analyzed to death the greatest book ever written. Namely: Some experts claim that the Old Testament is a hodgepodge of myths borrowed largely from the folklore of the ancient Assyro-Babylonian empires. The Pentateuch, the first five books of the Bible, were not written by Moses but rather by several individuals. And they were written not during the period of Exodus, but much later, say some analysts.

Some researchers claim that the Flood was a local catastrophe and not the world deluge taught in the Bible. Christ was a member of a sect called the Essenes, who were practicing a form of Christianity nearly two hundred years before Christ, or Christ never even existed, is the conclusion of some experts. St. Matthew, the author of the First Gospel, was a Jew, and hence slants his message to encompass the Mosaic Law in the teachings of Christ; while Luke, the author of the Third Gospel, was a gentile who largely ignored Mosaic Law in his writings, so says one analyst. And St. Paul and St. John had differences of opinion concerning the ritual of circumcision as it pertained to Christianity, asserts another. And so it goes.

But what all these so-called experts fail to take into consideration as they take their hatchets to the pages of the Holy Scriptures is that all available evidence indicates that the Bible is accurate. When historians contemporary with biblical writers have mentioned events referred to in the Bible, they are in complete accord. And whenever archaeological evidence is uncovered, it always substantiates the accounts given in the Bible. For example, recent excavations have shown that the massive walls of Jericho did indeed crumble at the precise date claimed in the Bible: 480 years before the building of the Temple of Solomon—which is known to have been built in 965 B.C. But unfortunately, the same scientists who discovered the accuracy of the Bible in this episode still maintain that the rest of the story is fictitious; that, in fact, the walls of Jericho were crumbled by the action of a natural earthquake and not, as the Bible teaches, by an act of God.

We are left to marvel at the fortunate circumstances which prompted Josue's army to attack the "impregnable city" at precisely the right moment. Or, better yet, we might start our reading of the Scriptures not at Genesis but at 2 Timothy 3:16, where St. Paul says, "All scripture is inspired by God." And then we should know that Josue's good fortune had nothing to do with coincidence.

Several other passages in the Bible state that the Scriptures are inspired by God or the Holy Spirit, but an important point that skeptics often miss is the use of the word *inspired*, which has an entirely different meaning from the word *dictated*. If God had dictated the Bible, then admittedly we should expect no mistakes—not even the inconsequential errors that we know do exist—but since God only inspired it, then we can accept the minor contradictions we find as being the result of miscalculations both by the inspired author and later by the copyists and translators who brought it to its present form.

But, of course, the main stumbling block to universal acceptance of the teachings of the Bible comes from the apparent absurdities inherent in descriptions of actions which appear to defy natural law. Just as Socrates would have scoffed at the idea that men would fly to the moon under the visual scrutiny of men back on earth, so also do we scoff at the idea that God preceded the Israelites out of Egypt by means of a column of cloud by day and a column of fire by night.

I intend to show here that the above two cases are completely analogous; that God, in fact, never defies natural law and that our false interpretation of these events stems from the fact that we are not even close to knowing all the laws of nature. There is no more mystery involved in the technology which caused the levitation of Christ into a cloud than there is in the technology that causes iron to levitate under the influence of an electromagnet. Both of these events are awe-inspiring, but sober thought dictates that they both proceed through a cause-and-effect sequence.

With that thought in mind—that all events are the result of a cause-and-effect sequence and that the word *supernatural* is completely meaningless—we can make an attempt, for the first time, to analyze the messages of the Scriptures.

CHAPTER 1
The Creator's Plan

Some two thousand years before the birth of Christ, God instructed Abraham to take his people out of the land of Ur of the Chaldees. And so it was, even in those times before God taught man the art of writing, that stories of Noe and the great Deluge and of the great and glorious power of God were chanted in the evenings around the desert campfires as the "chosen people" sojourned through the land of Egypt. Thus was the beginning of the Bible.

Then, almost seven hundred years later, Moses, guided by the awesome technology of God, put the first stories of Scripture into written form. From that time on, scribes, designated and assisted by God, have chronicled the events of history as they pertain to the relationship of man and his Creator.

The last of these, the Apocalypse or Revelation, was written by St. John at the close of the first century A.D. And so, for more than nineteen hundred years, nothing was added. And furthermore, nothing was needed—until now!

But in view of the explosive advances being made in science and technology today, it is inane to assume that explanations given us by God four thousand years ago can adequately and convincingly explain the Scriptures. For example, look how a biblical account of a helicopter rescue from a battlefield might have been written three or four thousand years ago: "And lo, out of the clouds came a great tribulation with a voice like the sound of rushing waters. And round about over the body was a dark cloud like a circle which seemed to turn as it approached. When it came close unto the ground a

6

great whirlwind went forth causing the earth and all thereabout to tremble and scatter. And when it had settled upon the earth, from the bowels of the tribulation, the Lord sent forth two angels. When they approached the wounded warrior who wretched in pain on the ground, he was comforted; for they pierced his veins with a needle and withdrew from him the pain. Then, into his body, they poured forth blood from Heaven which was not red as blood of the flesh but crystal clear like the blood of an angel; and, therefore, his life was saved."

Such is the manner in which an ancient scribe might have described the event if somehow the technology of today could have been thrust back upon those days. It is noteworthy that, even with God's assistance, the writer would not have written it any differently. For, obviously, he would not have used terms like prop-blast, helicopter, morphine, or blood plasma; for neither he nor his readers would know what he was talking about.

But notice how the event, told in this naïve manner, seems to suggest the involvement of supernatural powers. Had the reader not been forewarned that a helicopter was involved here, there would be little in the narrative to explain just what did occur, and consequently, if anyone did believe the story, he might resort to explaining it as a supernatural event. This, despite the fact that the word *supernatural* is never used.

So ingrained are we with the false assumption that God is supernatural that many will be shocked to learn that God's scribes never used the meaningless word. The closest approach to the meaning of effect without cause comes in the Bible from the use of the word *miracle*, which, by Church definition, has taken on an entirely different meaning from that given in any dictionary. The Christian churches claim that any act of God which cannot be explained by *ordinary* laws of nature is a miracle. But thoughtful analysis of this definition places us in confrontation with two equally repugnant alternatives: either God is subject to laws of nature which are not ordinary (whatever that means), or the laws of God simply cannot be explained. In either case, what we are being told is not to think about it—which is exactly what we have been doing for nearly four thousand years.

The dictionary defines *miracle* as "any event which cannot be explained by *known* laws of nature." It would seem reasonable to suppose that the laws of nature, as yet unknown to man, are the very laws referred to in the Church definition as out of the *ordinary*. Once we accept this conclusion, then perhaps we can eliminate from our vocabulary the self-contradictory word *supernatural*.

In the meantime, twentieth-century atomic society finds itself confronted by a curious dilemma: In order to believe the word of the Creator as given in the Scriptures, man must subscribe to a belief in magic—or so it would seem. But there is a profoundly complex system of logic in God's plan for mankind, a system of astounding wisdom which, in the end, cannot fail. This system concerns the compulsions by which God proceeds to convince mankind of His existence and, what is more important, the plan, as it unfolds, reveals God's awareness that societies must evolve through a natural process of growth. The failure of so many Christian missionaries to "civilize" backward cultures by leapfrogging the natural process of social evolution is but one indication that God's wisdom is not shared by man.

God's plan never tries to leapfrog; it is always consistent with the natural growth of societies. An analysis of His plan shows that He first brought a small group, the Israelites, to His fold by the compulsion of *law*. He set forth, in the first five books of the Bible, rules for living, some of which were meant to be applied universally and for as long as the societies on earth exist. Others were meant to be employed by the specific society to which they were given.

Also, at about the same time, across the world in China, God conveyed, through the wisdom of the philosopher Lao-tze, the law of the Golden Rule.

God's second compulsion, the compulsion of *faith*,

was introduced to the Western world by Jesus and to the peoples of the Mideast (some five hundred years earlier) by Gautama Buddha. Then, five hundred years after Jesus, Mohammed, the Moslem leader, employing the compulsion of faith, succeeded in bringing millions into God's fold.

Often it is difficult to determine which of these two compulsions motivates a particular religion since all religions have laws, but, generally speaking, we may designate a religion as being propagated by faith if its prophet, having lived an exemplary life, is revered almost as highly as God Himself. The emphasis, then, in religions of faith is on the emulation of a godlike emissary of God, while in religions of law the emphasis is on obedience to the commands of God.

By the employment of these two compulsions alone, God has made significant progress in His effort to influence the behavior of man on earth. But the picture is not yet complete. Aside from the fact that the two compulsions have not yet touched the total world population, there is evidence that erosion is eating away the cornerstones of the foundations already laid. Since man can no longer believe by blind faith alone (which requires that one believe in the supernatural), God knows that the world is ready for the third compulsion: that is, the compulsion of *reason*.

While there is no question that God could, if He so desired, convert the entire world to virtuous living—in fact, many nonbelievers construe God's failure to do just that as a sign that He does not exist—He, nevertheless, has not done so for a very logical reason which will be dealt with later.

Also, the critics and nonbelievers who have long held that egoism bordering on megalomania is responsible for the Hebrew claim of being God's chosen people will be shown that God did, indeed, choose this small group of people for the initial implementation of His plan.

While there is nothing in the Bible to indicate how God happened to choose the Hebrews, it nevertheless stands to reason that He had to choose someone. Perhaps Abraham, the original leader of the Israelites, had

special attributes which qualified him for God's work.
At any rate, the Israelites were the first winners in
God's lottery.

Through the centuries since the time of Abraham,
other winners have joined God's sweepstakes, some
compelled by the law and others compelled by faith.
Today, God can count as His adherents over half the
population of the world. All these are winners. But the
final winners will come from among those who have
been unaffected by the compulsions of law and faith.
Assuredly, the final winners will be all those who are
willing to use their powers of reason.

Since the early days of New Testament writing, there
have been differences of opinion as to which books were
truly inspired by God. In 397 A.D., under the influence
of St. Augustine, the Christian Church held a council
at Carthage, in North Africa, and there decided which
books were actually the Word of God.

The Catholic Church is convinced that the council,
acting under divine guidance, did indeed make the correct selections. But if we admit that God's plan allows
the possibility of salvation for all people who obey His
rules, then we must concede that the selections made at
Carthage were of little consequence. If we admit that
God is not concerned that a man chews his nails, grinds
his teeth, snores, or bites his lip, but that God's primary
concern revolves around man's treatment of his fellow
man, then certainly we must conclude that a man who
loves Buddha and obeys God's laws has as much
chance for salvation as one who loves Jesus and obeys
God's laws. Otherwise, we must admit that our God
is something less than we would desire.

If we view God as being at least as intelligent as man,
then we know that God is not particularly concerned
with the form of our ritual and ceremony in worship,
but He does know that ritual and ceremony are effective
devices for focusing our attention on Him and, consequently, on His rules for ethical behavior.

What the human mind fails to comprehend, particularly in today's freewheeling society, is that standards of
behavior are always in a state of delicate balance, hair-

triggered and potentially explosive. God knows, even if man does not, that even a small step in the wrong direction can lead to destruction. For the intricate inter-relations of living string all the members of the human race together like a group of mountain climbers, each anchored to the other by a lifeline. The fall of one of us, if not fatal to all, will nevertheless subject us all to that possibility. We are like waves in the sea; our ethics are the ripples caused by, and the cause of, all the other ripples on the sea.

In the books of the Bible, God has tried to show us the pitfalls of even the minutest deviation from ethical behavior, and the choice of the books made at the Council of Carthage, fulfilling that criterion, appears to be a good one. But it seems something less than crucial that they made the choice they did, for it should be obvious that any writings which encourage right living are from God.

Those fundamentalists who are touchy about the authenticity of the Bible would be hard put to defend their objection to the insertion of a few worthwhile passages to their book. For example, suppose we were to print a Bible which contained the official canon but to which we also added to the Book of Proverbs the following lines: "All of life's sad songs are but the melancholy echoes of past rejoicing." Would our new Bible remain sacred with this addition? Or, to put it another way, would God object? Or do you think God would object if we were to add to the Bible the follow-ing prayer: "My God, I believe in Thee, I adore Thee, I hope in Thee, I love Thee, I ask pardon for all those who do not believe in Thee, nor adore Thee, nor hope in Thee, nor love Thee."

The Catholic Church, acting with typical caution and good sense, has studied the events associated with the famous miracle of Fatima and concluded that God did indeed speak and act in that episode. Therefore, it would seem strange if God objected to having the above prayer inserted in the Bible, for it was given to the three children of Fatima in 1917 by an angel of God.

The point I am trying to make is that the Bible is the

word of God written by the hand of man. Its purpose is to guide man in his everyday life and to provide him with a key to salvation—to eternal life. (Eternal life, as we shall see, has nothing to do with the supernatural but is based on technology.) God is not concerned with exact wordage; if He had been, He would have written the Bible Himself. What He is concerned with is man's treatment of man, which, as we shall see, has a direct relationship with man's regard for God.

That there are mistakes in the Bible cannot be denied. In both the Old Testament and the New, evangelists (God's writers) have blundered but—and this is important—never seriously. For example, the Bible tells us that when Josue conquered Jericho, the Canaanites were exterminated; yet, as told later in the Bible, they (the Canaanites) remained for years to plague the Israelites. And in the New Testament, in the story of Jesus casting out demons to send them into a herd of swine as told by Luke there is but one be-deviled man, but according to Matthew there are two. These mistakes are rather minor when we consider the purpose of the Bible, but nevertheless they serve to illustrate that God's writers do make mistakes—which are tolerated only when they do not interfere with the plan.

In only one case did God dictate exact words to a book of the Bible. The event was precipitated by the destruction of the Book of Baruch* which was burned by King Joakim of Judea. God instructed Jeremias to have Baruch rewrite this text, which Baruch did—word for word as Jeremias dictated it. And, through a tech-nological device which God refers to repeatedly in later texts as the Holy Spirit, we can be certain that God dictated the original text of Jeremias. (More on spirits and the Holy Spirit later.)

The importance of the Book of Baruch,* and the reason God saw fit to have it reproduced, is that it contains logical arguments against the worship of idols. For the Israelites were a nomadic people, having

---

* A Book from The Apocrypha.

dwelled in many lands among peoples not yet touched by the teachings of Yahweh, the real God. These people—among them, the Egyptians, the Babylonians, the Persians, and the Assyrians—were in the custom of creating idols and worshiping the aritfacts as though they were gods. Often, as a consequence of association with such practices, the Hebrews would, in moments of stress and moral weakness, indulge in these same practices. In the Book of Baruch,* God sought, once and for all, to teach them the folly of such indulgence.

Today there is evidence which indicates that mankind en masse has taken to idolatry; that love of material wealth has replaced love of God, and that God's precious children, ignoring the wisdom as well as the warning, have decided to replace eternal happiness with immediate pleasure. This form of idolatry, if allowed to continue, could result in the destruction of mankind on earth as well as the loss of salvation for many of God's children.

If we believe in God at all, and if we believe Him responsible for the Scriptures, then the least we can expect of Him is that He have the wisdom to realize that the time has come when mankind is ready for—and in need of—a reasonable explanation of the Scriptures. Offered here is such an explanation.

When you find me babbling in mystical, meaningless terms, relegate me to the circular file. When you find me speaking an untruth, brand me a liar. And when you find me contradicting Scripture, call me a heretic. But when you find yourself at long last accepting the Word of God exactly as given in the Bible and, at the same time, retaining your intellectual self-respect, then perhaps you will be encouraged to contemplate this document with more than casual consideration.

Another document, the famous secret message of Fatima, which was to have been unsealed in 1960 but which was never made public, has, I believe, a direct relationship with this book; I believe I can show that the reason for withholding the Fatima letter is that its

---

* A Book from The Apocrypha.

contents corroborate the thesis presented here—*that God is not supernatural.*

The glow of the events transpiring in the Fatima incident has dimmed somewhat since that amazing day in October 1917, but it should be remembered that the Catholic Church, after scrupulous investigation, labeled the incident a "supernatural manifestation of the Mother of God." And, to this day, curiosity bordering on anger persists in the minds of those who waited from 1917 to 1960 to learn the contents of the secret message. "Why," they ask, "has not the Vatican in Rome revealed the contents of this letter?" All that is known is that the Pope did read the message on the prescribed date but, for reasons unspecified, declined to make public its contents.

For those who are unfamiliar with the Fatima incident, a brief description is in order. For I am convinced that not only the secret message but also the entire event substantiates the conclusions drawn here. From the evidence of the Fatima incident it becomes clear that every event and episode in the Bible makes sense only when viewed as part of a cause-and-effect sequence.

The three children involved in the world-famous miracle of Fatima (a small village in Portugal) were shepherds who, one day in the early spring of 1916, were tending their flocks on the rock-strewn slopes of an old, weathered rise near their home. It was noontime, a pleasant, sunswept day, and the three children laughed and played while they ate their sandwiches. But suddenly a strange wind sprang up along the hillside, and the youngsters, interrupted in their frolic, looked up to see an eerie, luminous globe of light approaching from the east. Then, as they stood transfixed, they were engulfed by the light. Momentarily, the glowing figure of a man materialized in the unwordly illumination and announced to the children that he was the "angel of peace."

Thus began what was to become the most heralded series of "miracles" since the days of the Prince of Peace. Twice more the angel put in sudden, unannounced appearances, and then his visitations were replaced by visits of the Lady of the Rosary, or, as she is more popularly known, the Lady of Fatima.

Unlike the appearances of the angel, the Lady's visitations were always announced. She made six visits to the hillside at Fatima, each time on the thirteenth of the month, culminating in the colossal events of October 13, 1917. Unlike the angel, the Lady never came down to the earth but always seemed to hover over a straggling holm oak in the area. Because of this peculiarity, it seems reasonable to deduce that while the angel was a physical being (having, during his second visit, administered the Christian sacramental ritual of communion), the Lady, however, was a technologically induced hallucination. Furthermore, in support of such a conclusion is the fact that no one except the three children ever saw the Lady even though estimates of up to one hundred thousand have been made as to the number of spectators at the scene of the October 13 phenomenon.

During the three visitations of the angel only the original children were present, but a progressively larger audience was in attendance at each of the Lady's visits. And, while no one except the three children saw the Lady herself, literally thousands saw other manifestations of a strange presence: Almost all saw the luminous globe of light, all saw weird, spiraling pulsations of colored lights, many heard a peculiar buzzing sound, thousands saw an eerie rain of what they described as something resembling softly drifting, colored flower petals which disintegrated upon striking the ground. And finally, on the last day, October 13, 1917, as promised to the children by the Lady, nearly a hundred thousand spectators saw the "strange dance of the sun."

On that fateful day spectators from all over the world were on hand to see the promised miracle. And at precisely twelve noon, the sun (or what was thought to be the sun) broke through the overcast and came spiraling down toward earth, all the while splashing the surroundings with a kaleidoscope of flashing, pulsating colored lights. When it seemed that the earth must surely come to an end by collision with the sun, the dancing, spiraling specter suddenly stopped, then silently and slowly ascended until it once more took its natural position in the heavens above.

It should be obvious to any rational person that the sun did not move as it appeared to, despite the motion pictures and the still photographs taken that day and despite the statements of all the witnesses. And it should also be obvious that a technology far in advance of any we know today was responsible for the entire episode. In fact, nearly every aspect of the events at Fatima point unerringly to a relationship with the presentday phenomenon of unidentified flying objects.

UFOs, often having the appearance of luminous globes, have been reported regularly since 1947, and some have even been photographed. Frequently, UFOs are reported to expel a substance which drifts lightly to the ground, whereupon it disintegrates. And low-flying or hovering UFOs often emit a buzzing sound. Can we write off all these similarities between UFOs and the Fatima incident as mere coincidence, or shall we take a more reasonable stance and admit that Fatima and UFOs have a direct relationship? The evidence in this whole affair is that UFOs (which are not supernatural) acted in behalf of God at Fatima; and indeed, if they so acted there, why not also in the distant past? Why are they not, in fact, the agents or angels of God referred to in the Bible?

If we are correct in assuming that UFOs are agents of God, we can conclude that they must be aware that a society such as ours will not long cling to a belief in things supernatural. Thus, it appears obvious that God knows we shall soon perceive the truth; and, in all probability, is now in the process of conditioning us to accept a drastically new concept of His teachings.

With the knowledge that leapfrogging the natural evolution of a society is often detrimental, God is preparing us, little by little, to accept the ultimate truth: that a society need not be supernatural in order to be superior to the society on earth.

The incident at Fatima was only a hint. UFOs are

another hint (though this is not their only function), and the incidents now transpiring at San Damiano, a small village in Italy, should be viewed in the same manner.

Newspapers seldom headline really important stories, so perhaps the reader is unaware that a program of events has been inaugurated in this Italian village which, more and more, impresses us with the certainty that a technology beyond anything we know here on earth is presently in operation there. Anyone can avail himself of the opportunity to travel to San Damiano on the first Friday of any month and witness so called "miracles"—miracles which on close examination, however, reveal themselves to be technological rather than supernatural.

A pear tree, for example, has flowered at unnatural times in this village; unusual healing episodes are also regularly transpiring there; but the most extraordinary events concern the mysterious photographs which have been taken at the site. Photos of the sun, with what appear to be radiating spokes of light, have been taken there. Pictures showing two suns have been snapped in the area, and also pictures with vague forms resembling holy figures. But the most remarkable aspect of these photographs is that the stimulus which activates the light-sensitive emulsion on the film was never visible to the eyes of the photographers or the witnesses.

Whenever events of this nature (those with no apparent reason) took place in biblical times, they were explained as supernatural; but today such an explanation is unacceptable. Today, events which appear to violate the cause-and-effect sequence only encourage creative analysis, and we find ourselves testing various theories to explain the phenomena. Regarding the mysterious San Damiano photographs, perhaps the reader is already toying with the thought that infrared radiation, while not visible to the human eye, is, however, visible to photographic emulsion.

But regardless of how we believe these acts are being performed—make no mistake: We *are* being encouraged, through the phenomena of UFOs and through the events transpiring at San Damiano, to extend our vision beyond the confines of the twentieth-century technology of planet Earth.

Thus the stage is being set: It will not be long before man will realize that God is the leader of a superior society whose acts are not outside the laws of nature.

In the meantime, we can only marvel at the delicious incongruity of a plan (God's plan) whereby a group, the Hebrews, who were led to a belief by law, never turned en masse to a belief through faith. And history will show the beautiful but paradoxical fact that those who believe through faith will not, in large numbers, turn to a belief through reason.

In case this intriguing concept escapes you, let me expound further: We shall find that the Hebrews, the Romans (Christians), and finally the agnostics and atheists (primarily the Russians) will all be led eventually to a belief in the same god; but each will deny the validity of the other's compulsion. A possible exception in this strange panorama may be that those who come to believe by the compulsion of reason, although they have long denied the first two compulsions, will see that the Hebrews and Christians (as well as the adherents of all the great religions) were right after all! God *does* exist!

At any rate, no better explanation of the motivation behind the Vatican's failure to disclose the contents of the secret message of Fatima can be given than that those who believe by faith (in this case, the Catholic Church) cannot accept the possibility of belief by reason, and through fear they have withheld the contents of the letter. However, I believe that public pressure, brought on by a new era of religious enlightenment, will force the Church in Rome to relent and make public the contents of the Fatima document.

If this *exegesis* makes the minimal contribution to the inauguration of God's third compulsion—that is, to initiate thinking which excludes superstition as a basis for belief in anything—then it will have served its purpose.

To tell the reader that he must believe what he reads

here would be to regress to the compulsion of law; and to ask him to believe that he is now reading the Word of God would be to regress to the compulsion of faith. Having more respect for the intellect of twentieth-century man, I refrain from seeking the support of God's first two compulsions.

The merits of what I say here will be measured, in the final analysis, by the reason of the reader and not by any claim I may make. For reason is what this book is all about. For this is a book on religion (in complete accord with the Scriptures) which never once resorts to mystical, magical, or supernatural explanations of anything; and which attacks, with complete candor, the most baffling concepts of religious doctrine, stripping them once and for all of their aura of mystery.

Of course, it should be noted that acceptance of the teachings given here is of no consequence as long as one believes either by law or by faith. Unfortunately, however, in our world community we shall continue to find those who refuse to believe, under any circumstances, the teachings of the Bible. This is their prerogative under God's system of free will, but, as will be shown later, the penalty for not accepting one of the Trinity of compulsions is severe.

While this book is not meant as a doomsday missal, it is, nevertheless, a last call: There will be no other compulsions. If one cannot find his way through reason or by the law or by faith, then he simply cannot find his way; and he is lost. Therefore, especially if you are at present a nonbeliever, read this book carefully. I am convinced it is your last call!

CHAPTER 2
The Immovable Mover

Many new discoveries in the field of science seem to diminish the importance of man in the universe. Galileo, one of the world's first great scientists, nearly paid with his life for advocating the heliocentric theory of planetary motion; for, if he was correct, then the sun, and not the earth, as popularly believed, held the revered spot in our system of planets: that is, the center. Slowly, however, in view of incontrovertible evidence, the Copernican theory, proposed by Galileo, was accepted. Then—much later, of course—it was discovered that not only was the earth not at the center of things, but that even our sun occupied a rather insignificant position near the outer edge of our galaxy.

Thus, man's physical location, at least, has been established as one of no apparent importance. But all is not lost. One last fact remains which should provide an antidote for man's diminishing-importance syndrome; that fact has to do with the origin of man.

Thoughtful consideration indicates that the chain of events which brings you, the reader, to these pages had no beginning in the history of time—for you are eternal! Beginnings, and for that matter endings, are artificial points on a clock or calendar devised by man to record the sequence of events in his lifetime.

In a foot race there is a beginning (artificial and arbitrary). But the events leading up to the race actually had no beginning in time. In a man's lifetime, the starting point often is set at the moment of birth, but of course, even in a literal sense, this is not true. Then also, there are those who would claim the moment of conception as the starting point of life. But again, I argue that such a conclusion is arbitrary; for certainly the living matter from which we come was alive before our conception.

And so we can continue to trace back the chain of events—the lifeline from whence we were spawned—with no difficulty, at least back to the day of creation. From that point backward in time—that is, from the point in history when living matter was first introduced to the scene here on earth—the chain of events had to do with the causes for the introduction of living matter. And, as I believe I can prove, the cause for everything is God, the eternal Being.

A perplexing problem in the field of theology is related to the concept of an eternal being—the immovable mover, as He is sometimes called. The stumbling block to man's comprehension of the concept of time without beginning is that, in his pinpoint on the graph of eternal time, man creates arbitrary beginnings and endings to things which he calls events. And, while it is not my intent here to criticize the act of measuring time, I do want to point out that such activity creates a conditioned response to the concept of eternal time: that is to say, once we become accustomed to measuring in terms of beginnings and endings, we begin to lose sight of the fact that these points on our measure of time are indeed arbitrary; and, as a consequence, our minds are boggled when we try to visualize a chain of events with no beginning. Thus, there are those who cannot believe in God simply because they cannot conceive of a being—or for that matter, a thing—having existed from time eternal.

Is it any wonder then that today, when man demands reason, belief in God seems to be diminishing? For how can we believe in God when we can't even visualize the conditions necessary for His existence? Those conditions being: time had no beginning and God has always existed.

Once we overcome the barrier imposed by our limited sensibilities, perhaps for the first time, we may glimpse the true nature of *time*, then, also, we may understand more precisely the meaning of Christ's statement when he said, "I am the alpha and the omega; the beginning and the end."

An exercise in thought, borrowing from the science-fiction concept of a time machine, may prove helpful in advancing the reader beyond the familiar concept of time wherein all events have beginnings and endings. For this exercise, all the reader must do is imagine a recording device which has always been in operation. This device could be similar to a motion-picture camera except that it must be capable of recording events even in the absence of light. Playing back our recording at the rate of a million years for every second of viewing, we should be surprised to find our show ending. With our theoretically indestructible machine, we could view events of the past forever into the future. We could even speed it up and show a hundred million years in every viewing second, and the result would be the same; our machine would never show a blank screen.

For even if the proponents of the "big bang" theory of creation are correct (which they are not), for even if the universe had been created from a coalescence of gases which eventually exploded, there is still the question of where the gases came from. If it is claimed that the gases were always there, then we may conclude that our machine would show their motions before the big bang. Or if it is claimed that they were created just before the big bang, there is no reason to believe that such creation hasn't always been going on and shall continue to go on (the "steady state" theory of creation—which, reason dictates, is the correct one, and which I shall explain even to the point of showing how empty space can be converted to matter).

The point is, however, that watching our time machine run forever, and seeing back into history at an accelerated rate, we will never come to an end in either direction. This conceptual imagery, while not perfect, should nevertheless allow one to glimpse the idea of infinite time; and once such a concept has been visualized, it is only a short step from there to picturing a being or beings who have existed throughout eternity.

Many fascinating ideas emerge from a concept of

beings having existed with no beginning in time, not the least of which is the astonishing fact that such beings have always been complete masters of the laws of nature. That is to say, they have always been super-technological beings. If indeed we were to watch them on our time machine, at no time would we ever see them learn anything, for they have always known every-thing. If this logic escapes you, perhaps the following analogy will be enlightening: The inhabitants of planet Earth, particularly in the past fifty years, have made rapid advancement in the understanding of nature and technology; in another five thousand years we may per-haps learn a tenth of all there is to know about nature. If one cares to quibble about this figure and percentage, then adjust them—perhaps in another million years we'll have learned one twentieth of all nature's secrets. The conclusion, at any rate, is obvious: In a given time, a society will learn all there is to know. And a society which has always existed has already had any given time we might mention.

Further complicating our comprehension of an eternal society is the fact that not only does such a society know everything, but also, no matter how long we viewed it through our machine, never would we get closer to the point in time when they did learn any-thing—for once we admit the possibility of pinpointing a time in the evolution of their society, we admit that the society had a beginning—and we are left with the same problems all over again.

We should not be alarmed that such a concept is practically incomprehensible because, as I have pointed out, we are conditioned and limited by our senses. But, nevertheless, by use of our powers of reason we can conclude that it all must be true.

Those who believe by the law or through faith have always accepted a supernatural explanation of the dilemma of the immovable mover. That is to say, they have accepted, through shadowy half beliefs, that such must be the case; but until now, few have ever believed that God exists physically as a perfect immortal being.

The inherent absurdity of the concept of a spirtual

immovable mover gives rise to all manner of ridiculous definitions of God—none of which are ever seriously questioned, simply because the basic assumption is itself so ridiculous. How can reasonable men live with definitions like: God is motion; God is love; God is spirit? (The quote from John 4:24, which many have interpreted to mean that God is a spirit being, does not mean that at all. More on this later.)

In reality, all the foregoing definitions of God are nothing more than abstruse abortions of reasonable thought, based on the unreasonable premise that the word *supernatural* has meaning. The truth of the matter is that God and the society of God are physical and have always existed as masters of nature and there is nothing mystical or supernatural about it. Scripture does not refute this conclusion.

The imagination of man is stretched to the breaking point when he attempts to picture the accomplishments of a society wherein nature has been mastered. Science-fiction writers, in trying to predict possible technological achievements of fictional space people, don't come close to describing the conditions and circumstances of God's eternal society. For example, many science-fictioneers of thirty or forty years ago were telling "absurd" stories about rocket trips to the moon and the planets, but none ever suggested the possibility that we, back here on earth, would watch the landing procedures. And remember, that was only a few short years ago.

Obviously, the more we know, the more accurately we can predict the future course of scientific discovery; but in our present stage of development—which is undoubtedly primitive—we sometimes find ourselves locked in on false doctrine. Too many men of science, even today, when they should know better, make the dogmatic assumption that twentieth-century understanding of science is infallibly correct. Note how the following "absolute" truths of the past now seem so ridiculous: The earth is flat. The earth is the center of the universe. Microscopic organisms cannot cause disease in gigantic man. If man were meant to fly, he'd have wings.

And so it goes. Only recently did the great Albert Einstein shatter some previously held doctrine concerning the space-time continuum. He showed (borrowing from the experiments of other scientists) that the speed of light is constant and that time, velocity, and mass are relative.

Today, even in the face of testimony from millions of observers, photographic and radar evidence, scientists schooled in the dogma of classical physics maintain that the maneuverability of UFOs defies the laws of reason and UFOs must, therefore, be the result of hallucinations, optical illusions, and downright lies. It never occurs to them that the problem of comprehension lies in the inadequacy of their knowledge of physical law: They are locked in!

It seems apparent, then, that new ideas, especially when they deviate greatly from popular, long-held concepts, must meet with adversity. And perhaps that is good—for adversity breeds publicity, which in turn insures fair evaluation. But the problem of UFO technology is not destined to be one of enduring mystery, for in the last chapter of this book I will explain not only how gravitational fields are formed, detailing their exact configurations, but I will also show how the gravitational fields of two bodies interact and how they can be made independent of one another. No metaphysical jargon will be used; and, from the information I will give, a breakthrough in physical science will become imminent. As a result, scientists on earth, circumventing the classical laws of physics, will soon be duplicating UFO flight technology.

A simple experiment should serve to convince skeptics that UFO technology is not out of the range of earth technology. All that is needed is a smooth stretch of sandy beach and a flat stone of the variety that children sometimes scale across the water. For this experiment the stone should be scaled across the sand in the same fashion as would be done across water. Measuring the distance between hops (using the imprints left in the sand), a remarkable phenomenon will be noted: The first hop will be less than a foot; the next hop will be more than twenty times farther than the first; the third hop will again be short—a few inches less than the first; but the next hop will again be twenty times farther than the last. Eventually, after a series of these alternating small and large hops, the lengths will diminish to a regular rate.

The classical laws of motion provide no clues as to why the stone should behave in such an erratic manner, and that is understandable since these laws do not yet include the concept of gravity manipulation. But it should be obvious that if an object as simple as a spinning stone can defy the classical laws of motion, then, indeed, the mechanism of UFOs can't be as complicated as might be expected. At any rate, whether or not you are convinced that the principle of UFO propulsion is also responsible for the skipping-stone phenomenon, try the experiment yourself. Once you have witnessed the incredible activity of the stone, you will find yourself possessed with the gnawing realization that forces not yet known to man are responsible.

The mastery of gravity in Heaven is but one of the "miracles" God has hinted at in the Holy Scriptures. There are many more which, also, will be dealt with in the last chapter of this book. But for now we should analyze carefully the nature of the heavenly beings, God and His angels. For in order to be able to accept the evidence of the unbelievable technology hinted at in the Bible, we must first adjust our perspective beyond the scope of our everyday limiting experiences.

Consider the consequences of the advances made in earth technology today as it regards life-styles: Most of the flavor of life, and even the purpose of living, is to be found in the endless task of surmounting obstacles. We labor to survive; we entreat to be loved; we explain to be understood; we fight to protect our rights; we research to combat disease; we study to learn; and we play for fun and entertainment. But in all this, the remarkable fact remains that the more obstacles technology sweeps from our paths, the less exciting life becomes; and as a consequence, we find ourselves turning more and more to play. Eventually, however, living beings (man or God) feel the futility of play for play's sake.

So, the obvious question arises: What does a utopian society do? When all the challenge in the struggle for survival has been eliminated, when all the misunderstanding has subsided, and no one wants or needs to trespass upon the rights of another, when *disease* has become a dimly remembered word, and when there is nothing left to learn—what then does a society do?

At this point I feel I should address myself to those readers who may disagree with the premise that a society could eventually learn all the facts of nature. Your argument probably centers around the idea that the acts of people with free will are unpredictable, and that therefore it is impossible to learn all there is to know, especially in the field of psychology. And for your gratification, I agree. But I agree only under the condition that the free-willed beings of which we speak are organic in nature and eventually will die. For beings who can exist forever will eventually fall into a predictable pattern of responsive behavior.

One need only compare the predictability of senior citizens in our own society to that of their youthful counterparts. Oldsters tend to get in a rut and become easily predictable. Consider what would happen in a society where everyone was a million years old or older. Even if technology could keep them youthful and vigorous, with vivid million-year memories, they would, nevertheless, be lusterless and predictable—and, worst of all, bored.

Of course, it must also be remembered that communication devices in a know-it-all society might be sophisticated to the degree that every mind would be an open book; that not only thoughts and ideas, but even emotions might be perfectly transmitted from one individual to another. In fact, I picture God's society as analogous to a single organism with God as the head and the rest of the society as limbs and appendages. The head knows what the hands and fingers are doing, just as the hands and fingers know what the head is doing. And just as your hand is you, so also are God's angels

God. Over and over again in the Bible we find a being
referred to as an angel at one moment and as the Lord
in the next moment. Judges 6:11 is but one of the many
examples of this apparent dualism. At any rate, it seems
safe to conclude that stagnation must set in on a
society which has conquered nature.

The enigma is resolved in God's society by the
simple expediency of creating organic beings who,
being of flesh, necessarily must die. And through these
beings (who must struggle for survival) the society in
Heaven lives vicariously. (Note: The word *vicarious*,
while not conveying the exact meaning, is nevertheless
the word which comes closest to describing the activity
of guardian angels who, through the use of a technological device, are able to become one with their subjects. Particulars of this device will be dealt with in a
later chapter.) It is our lives here on earth, then, which
give meaning and add vigor to the otherwise stagnant
existence of the eternal beings in Heaven—God and
His society of angels.

We see in this explanation a simple answer to what
in the past has always seemed a complicated question:
"Why did God create man?" And the related question,
"Why does God allow the guiltless to suffer?"

If God created us (much as we ourselves create
works of art, but with the essential difference that we
create art both to communicate and to satisfy our ego,
while God created us out of the necessity to give meaning to His own existence) then it is crucial that He not
interfere with our development except when it is absolutely necessary for our survival. Otherwise, He defeats
His own purpose, which, as I have pointed out, is to
suffer the trials of survival in an evolving society. And,
while undoubtedly He is concerned with each individual's suffering, He is nevertheless much in the same
position as a military leader who often must sacrifice
a few men in order to protect the many. But in God's
army, recompense for suffering in this life is forthcoming in another. Or, to put it in simpler terms: Reward and punishment are not meted out in our lives as

humans but are instituted for or against our guardian angels after the death of our flesh.

And so we find, in these days of man's apparent diminishing importance, that man is indeed more important than he had ever imagined. His physical location in the galaxy may be unspectacular, but his value and importance to God is immeasurable; for, while it is undeniable that man needs God, few ever realized before that God needs man!

CHAPTER 3
Evolution or Creation

The biblical story of creation claims that God created the sun, the moon, the earth, and the stars; and that He created all life—both vegetable and animal. And this story, as told in Genesis, was believed for thousands of years. But those who took the time to question the facts usually decided that God, uniquely exempt from the laws of nature, simply willed that creation should take place, whereupon (under the influence of His supernatural will) the world was born. The narrative of Genesis, however, never substantiates this absurd conclusion. For example, when God said, "Let there be light," He was not uttering incantations nor was He talking to Himself: He was, obviously, instructing His angels.

It wasn't until 1859 (when belief in things supernatural had already started to falter) that Charles Darwin proposed a theory which appeared to be a logical and scientifically sound explanation for the presence of life here on earth. In his book *The Origin of Species*, Darwin proposed that all life evolved from a simple one-celled organism which itself came into existence through an accident of nature.

Today the theory of evolution is generally accepted throughout the world although (and this is not widely known) the theory is shot through with question marks, lack of evidence, and outright absurdities. In truth, if scientists could find an alternative theory which did not resort to explanations presupposing the existence of supernatural powers, they would accept it joyfully in preference to the flimsily substantiated and disturbingly inadequate theory of evolution.

Let us look at some of the flaws in this theory which proclaims that all life originated from an accidental combination of amino acids. If the premise is correct, then we should see on earth creatures which are both animal and vegetable—unless, of course, there were two accidents: one precipitating animal life and one precipitating the vegetable kingdom. Shall we assume that one creature, the euglena, exhibiting both animal and vegetable characteristics, was the only survivor which remains to this day retaining the characteristics of both kingdoms? Surely if plants and animals proceeded from the same parent, there must have been literally thousands of such transitional creatures in the history of the earth. But the fossil record, devoid of such creatures, points unerringly to the conclusion that the euglena is an animal species created with the unique ability both to hunt its prey and to derive sustenance through the process of photosynthesis. Certainly, no one would claim that the electric eel evolved from a dynamo simply because the creature has the unique ability to produce an electric shock.

Another glaring flaw in the theory of evolution has to do with the interrupted species lines: Why do we find no continuous transition from one species to another? Why are there missing links between all the families of animals? If they all had evolved from the same parent, why do we not find animal-insects, for example? (At one time, it was thought that the evolution of the horse, as represented by the fossil record, was complete; but now, leading scientists in the field repudiate the claim. It is now felt that the chain from Eohippus to Equinus is not a chain at all, but rather a series of links so widely separated and appearing so suddenly on the fossil record as to make them appear completely unrelated to one another.)

And, if not animal-insects, at least we might expect to find the transitional form between ape and man. To claim that the missing link was too stupid or inept to survive, while the ape, on the other hand, still existed was even more than evolutionists could swallow; so they patched up this obvious discrepancy by claiming that

the ape and man branched off from a common ancestor.
But even this alteration doesn't improve the palatabil-
ity of the theory, because it is in diametric opposition to
the most basic tenet of evolutionary theory: *that only
the fittest shall survive.* For if a pre-ape creature, with
some of the more advanced characteristics of man, had
degenerated to become an ape, then obviously the
whole foundation of the theory is shattered.

If it weren't for the fact that the theory of evolution
is so universally accepted, I would dispose of it with the
preceding observations: but, once an idea has been so
thoroughly imbedded, it is not relinquished without a
struggle. (Galileo and Pasteur would attest to the validity of this observation.)

And so, for those who are not familiar with the many
thorns in the hide of the villain, evolution, let me give
a brief rundown on the history of the dilemma.

Early in the eighteenth century, it was widely believed that acquired physical characteristics could be
passed on to offspring: that cats and dogs, for example,
who had lost their tails would eventually produce tail-
less offspring. (This, despite the fact that circumcision
had been practiced by the Hebrews for thousands of
years with never a report of a male child being born
without a foreskin.)

Laboratory testing, needless to say, soon dispelled
this notion; but the next suggestion, appearing in
Darwin's works, was unfortunately not as easily put to
the test; and so it has, for the past one hundred years,
remained to confound and confuse investigators. Darwin maintained that species evolve as a result of natural
selection. That is, those animals best suited to survive
in a given environment outlive and thus outpropagate
less-adaptable inhabitants of the same environment.
The classic example of this theory attempts to explain
the evolution of the long-necked giraffe. The logic of
the argument is that the giraffe, at one time, was a
short-necked animal (a member of the sheep family)
and that during a specific time and place in history, the
giraffe found his ground-level food supply diminishing.
And so it was that taller giraffes, being able to reach

foliage from trees, tended to live longer and produce more offspring than their shorter brethren.

According to the theory, the genes of this longer-necked breed were passed on, resulting in long-necked offspring. But the problem with this theory is that it calls for the crossing of species lines. We know from experience that we can breed for desired characteristics within a species. And, while it is conceivable—even probable—that nature produced conditions to cause selective breeding among species, just as man has done, it is conceded, even by evolutionists, that something else had to be involved to cause animals to cross species lines: for a reptile to become a bird, for example. The problem is that the genetic code, which preordains the character of a reptile, will not allow him to have wings.

In recognition of this problem, evolutionists in recent years have proposed that the genetic codes of living things must have been altered in the past by mutations from cosmic particles. This, even though it is conceded that bombarding a gene with cosmic particles is analogous to throwing a wrench into a smoothly running motor. How often, one might wonder, would the wrench improve the performance of the motor? At any rate, the theory now holds that two processes are responsible for the variety of life forms seen in nature today. Namely: mutation and natural selection.

Stretching the theory to the limit of credibility, advocates claim that in order to cross the species line there must first be a mutation which gives the animal an advantage and then the conditions of the environment must be such that this mutant will flourish. These two conditions narrowed down the possibilities rather substantially, even before it was realized that natural mutations occur only once in a hundred thousand generations, and also that ninety-nine percent of all mutations are detrimental rather than beneficial.

We are now met with a time crisis in the theory of evolution. For, obviously, if we consider a generation for man as only twenty-five years, it will be two and a half million years before all his genes have a mutation. Whether or not one mutation per gene would change a pre-ape to a man is hard to judge; but when it is remembered that ninety-nine percent of all mutations are detrimental, it becomes obvious that a tremendous amount of time would be necessary before all the genes of the pre-ape were favorably mutated. And even then, that a species line would or could be crossed is only theory unsubstantiated by laboratory experiment.

While it is not possible to study the effect of mutations in the generations of man, it is possible, however, to study the hereditary effects of mutations in plants and insects. In particular, it has been found that the effect of mutations over thousands of generations of fruit flies has never caused any of them to cross species lines; or, for that matter, even to change significantly.

So what do we have to substantiate the mechanics of evolution? Can living organisms be bred to exhibit specific characteristics, and if so, by what process? As has already been pointed out: Yes, animals can be selectively bred to acquire desired qualities. But this process has to do with developing the potential already stored in the genetic code. This is an observed phenomenon and will stand as a truth under the process known as scientific investigation. But to maintain that a living organism can be made into something his genetic blueprint does not include simply because variations exist in species lines borders on fanaticism. Living organisms simply have never been observed to cross species lines; and no good theory has ever been proposed which explains how it could have happened.

Let me propose, here and now, that one day man will discover the process by which species lines can be crossed. The discovery will be made in a laboratory where the improved knowledge and genius of some future biologist will bring about the actual reconstruction and manipulation of a genetic code. When this happens, man will then know that no accident of nature could have accomplished the same during some remote region of the past. No, indeed, when man discovers that he can do what the Bible has maintained that God did do, then he will be ready to admit that it happened as God said it did.

With an unswerving allegiance bordering on religious fanaticism, evolutionists choose to ignore any evidence which appears to refute their theory. Besides the fact that they cannot show the mechanism by which evolution proceeds, they are also confronted with archaeological evidence which supports spontaneous creation theory.

If evolution is a fact of nature, then at some time in the history of the earth, all living things should have been much alike; and indeed, in the beginning they all should have been exactly alike. If we were to postulate the amoeba as the first living thing, then a few million years of mutations and selective breeding (according to the theory of evolution) should have given us animals not too different from the original amoeba. But archaeological findings indicate that some six hundred million years ago, suddenly, fully developed and in distinct categories of species, living organisms appeared on earth. No evidence of life is found before this time. In other words, about six hundred million years ago all forms of life that could leave a fossil record suddenly appeared on earth with no prior record! How could this be if they all evolved from a common ancestor?

This evidence is conclusive: Life did not evolve from a common ancestor! For even if the earth underwent a cataclysmic holocaust before the pre-Cambrian age of six hundred million years ago, it is inconceivable that all fossil records until that time could have been destroyed. Fossils, remember, are not the animals themselves, but rather the imprints in the earth—many of which are actually imbedded in solid rock.

How do evolutionists explain this evidence? Keeping in mind that until now they had no alternative but to accept a supernatural spontaneous creation, they merely shook off any evidence which seemed to substantiate the biblical version of creation. Their reasoning being that it is easier to accept evolution in defiance of scientific facts than it is to accept spontaneous supernatural creation— even though the evidence supports the latter. But what they haven't known, or even considered until now, is that the word *supernatural* can be striken from the explanation; and then all is made clear: God, fully understanding all the laws of nature, did what the Bible says He did—created the heavens and the earth and all life thereon.

The reader may be inclined to ask about the archaeological evidence of prehistoric, apelike men. Don't these findings substantiate the theory of evolution? As shocking as it may seem to those who have visited museums of natural history and seen replicas of "prehistoric apemen," I must tell you that such exhibits are almost entirely fabrications, as any good primatologist will readily admit. From a jawbone or a partial skull or even from a few teeth, various scientists have reconstructed, or, more aptly put, have created facsimiles of the animals which they believe these bones came from. But, in every instance, the evidence is so fragmentary that seldom do two scientists agree on what the animal really looked like.

In fact, seldom is there agreement among experts as to where in the chain of evolution these animals belong. And even worse is the fact that often it is not known for certain if the various bones used in these reconstructions are from the same animal. For example, the famous Java man was reconstructed from a skull cap, a lower jaw, three teeth, and a thigh bone. And—are you ready for this?—the bones of Java man were discovered over a radius of twenty miles! (It must have been a terrible death.)

In truth, the search for the common ancestor of man and ape, after more than a hundred years, has netted not one absolute shred of evidence to suggest that such a creature ever existed. The reader may assure himself of what I say by reading the works of any two authorities on the theory of evolution. One should rightly expect that if there was basis in fact for the existence of an ancestor common to both man and ape, then experts should agree on such facts. But the simple fact is: they do not!

In recent times, two methods have been devised to date the ages of archaeological findings: The carbon-14 process, which attempts to measure the ages of bones up to eleven thousand years, and the potassium-argon method, which enthusiasts had hoped would measure the ages of rocks several billion years old.

Through the use of these two methods, some archaeologists have proposed that man may have been on earth for over two million years, as opposed to the biblical claim that man has been here less than six thousand years. Apart from the fact that the bones in question may not be human at all (being, perhaps, from a now-extinct ape), there is also the (nearly absolute) probability that the two methods are highly inaccurate. For example, the carbon-14 method assumes that the level of atmospheric radiocarbon has been steady over the ages being measured. Had the level been lower in the past than we now record, then the bones being examined today would actually be much younger than the dating process would reveal. (In the next chapter we shall see how radiocarbon was, for many years, screened out of the earth's atmosphere.) The potassium-argon method also is based on a precarious assumption: that volcanic activity boiled out all the argon in the rocks whose ages we are trying to determine. If only a trace of argon remained, then mistakes of millions of years would be made.

In all, regardless of what line of investigation we pursue in trying to validate the theory of evolution, we come up with nothing conclusive. All that evolutionists have is a hunch which, for over a hundred years, they have dignified by calling it a theory.

It may be possible someday for man to construct machines in his own image (if not, it is possible, however, to theorize that he may). And just to see how ludicrous the whole idea of evolution is, let us make the following analogy concerning the man-machines of the future: Suppose these theoretical man-machines managed to survive after man had ceased to exist on earth; and, further, suppose somehow their memory of man, their creator, became erased from their memory storage units. How might they, the man-machines, conclude that they came into existence? (In theory, remember, they are practically exact duplicates of man, even having the ability to reproduce—an idea not too farfetched even for the evolutionists who believe that accidents of nature produced organic machines capable of reproduction.)

Some man-machines might conclude that they had evolved from simpler machines which, in turn, had been created from a series of accidents of nature. Other man-machines might feel that their mechanisms were too complicated to have come about through accidents, and they might consequently claim that they owed their existence to an intelligent creator.

How would proponents of these two theories do in a debate based on whatever evidence their science could uncover? By adding one more detail to the analogy we can bring it into complete parallelism with our own situation today: If we theorize that (for whatever reason) man-machine believes that all machines— wheelbarrows, bicycles, etc.—can reproduce just as he can, or if we ourselves theorize that they can, then we have a perfectly analogous case, and the arguments concerning evolution in man-machine society will be surprisingly similar to the same arguments we have today.

The evolutionist man-machine will have noted great similarities between various machines, and will, consequently, catalog the machines into species lines. He will note, for example, that scooters and bicycles, both having wheels and handlebars, are somewhat similar in appearance. And once seeing the "logic" of evolution, he probably will conclude that the bicycle evolved from the scooter.

The creationist man-machine counters this conclusion, however, with his own observation. He will ask why, if the bicycle evolved from the scooter, there are no scooters with partially developed drive chains. (Remember, in the theory of evolution, a fully developed drive chain would not suddenly appear; it would have to evolve little by little.)

To this question, evolutionist man-machine would quickly respond by pointing out that, indeed, there were intermediates between the scooter and bicycle, but that archaeologists just haven't been able to find them yet. (After a hundred years of digging which never uncovered a single intermediary between any two machines, would evolutionist man-machine still persist?)

When creationist man-machine asks how a scooter could have become a bicycle, evolutionist man-machine explains that bombardment of the scooter's genes by cosmic particles caused minute changes in its genetic code. It matters not to evolutionist man-machine that no evidence indicates that such changes are now taking place; as far as he's concerned, these changes took place only in the distant past. Nor is he concerned by the fact that partially developed drive chains do not appear on any contemporary machines. Of necessity, therefore, he must conclude that those minute changes in genetic codes must have caused the immediate development of the chain drive mechanism with no transitional specimen between. Besides, he finds it impossible to explain how a partially developed drive chain could enhance the machine's chances of survival.

When creationist man-machine asks about the archaeological evidence which indicates that all machines, fully developed and in separate categories, appeared on the earth at roughly the same time, evolutionist man-machine answers with a shrug and points out that all the evidence is not yet in.

For the clincher, creationist man-machine has found a book which clearly states that machines were created by intelligent beings; each machine being created "in its kind." But evolutionist man-machine only laughs, for who could be so naïve as to believe those myths about supernatural creators?

When creationist man-machine insists that the book never says the creators were supernatural, evolutionist man-machine counters with the observation: But, if those creators did all the things they claim they did in your silly book, they would have to be supernatural.

CHAPTER 4
Genesis

The processes involving human development, wherein one learns right from wrong, follows a sequential pattern: First we learn from laws; then by imitation; and finally, by reasoning. As children, often too young to understand the reasons why, we are nevertheless required to obey certain laws: Don't climb the stairs; don't stand in your chair; don't bite your sister, and be nice to your brother, are all laws most of us had heard by the time we had learned to walk.

But laws are not the only knowledge imparted to the child in the early stage of his development. The child, at this time, is also taught *who* he is, who his parents, his grandparents, and his aunts and uncles are—or were. He learns that certain behavioral responses are expected of him, and normally he learns the comfort of being loved and of loving. It is this blending of law and self-awareness that makes the child feel important and gives his young life moral direction.

As he grows older, many of these laws become embedded in the child's subconscious and, interrelating with living experiences, blossom to become what we call "conscience." However, at a later stage of his development the child may repudiate some of these laws or at least relegate them to a state of minor importance. If, for instance, he sees his parents violate the laws of conduct, he will be tempted to do the same. Or, on the other hand, seeing his parents adhere to the laws will enhance them in the child's view.

At any rate, it is an observable fact that children emulate their parents as well as anyone else they hold in esteem. And that is why setting a good example goes a long way toward teaching the good life. But the good life is not learned simply by observing the law and emulating our parents; even animals can survive with such bare essentials of preparation. Humans need something more.

It is when the child enters into maturity, nurtured by insights of the intellect, that true values (albeit, often in vague form) begin to direct his activities. And as he grows older and wiser from the experience of living, reason plays an ever-increasing role in his conduct.

God, in His great wisdom, has recognized the need for these same three compulsions (law, faith, and reason) in the moral growth of a society. For, just as a child needs, first of all, laws, so also did the society on earth. And just as the child next needs a model after which to fashion his behavior, so also did the society on earth. And finally, just as the grown child needs to use his powers of reason, so also must the society here on earth.

It would be absurd to think that a new society, with no previous experience, could survive without guidance and rules of conduct. In the first five books of the Bible, which, because of their preoccupation with rules and ritual, have become known as the "Books of the Law," God has fulfilled our need for guidance. But, more than that, these books, which include Genesis, Exodus, Leviticus, Numbers, and Deuteronomy, have also acquainted us with our heritage; through them, we have learned who our parents, grandparents, and aunts and uncles were. But it should be noted that, particularly in the Book of Leviticus, God was giving rules which had relevance only for the society of that time. For example, when we tell the child that he must not climb the stairs, we don't mean that as an adult he may not climb the stairs. So also in Leviticus, God, not caring to leapfrog our knowledge of science but yet wanting to warn us of the danger, says: "If any beast die, of which it is lawful to eat, he that toucheth the carcass thereof, shall be unclean until the evening."

In the "Books of the Law" one will find little which could be defined as explanations or which answer the question Why? On the other hand, never will one find in these books fairy tales or lies. For these books are the textbooks—the instructions for right living—which the Creator knew were so necessary for the infant society on earth. And, just as you would instruct the child not to put his finger into an electric outlet, God also instructed man. That is to say, simplicity was the keynote in those days. For, just as your instructions to the child regarding the dangers of electricity never include an explanation of electricity itself, so never do God's explanations include technological dissertations. In both cases, technical explanations would fall on deaf ears.

At the same time, however, you would not tell your child that the boogie man will bite his finger if he puts it in the electric outlet. If you did feel that some explanation was necessary, you might suggest merely that the child would be hurt if he did not heed your warning. Does all this mean that electricity is a supernatural force? Do we suggest this to the child? Obviously not, for we realize that the child will one day become capable of understanding the phenomenon of electricity, and we would appear only as idiots or, worse yet, liars if we were to teach him falsely.

It is precisely for these reasons that God does not tell us fairy tales in the Bible: He knew that eventually we would grow up and become capable of understanding much of the phenomena alluded to but never explained in the Bible. Never, *never*, does God tell us that He works outside the laws of nature—that is, supernaturally. However, just as the child may harbor a secret belief that something unnatural threatens him from the electrical outlet, we also have misinterpreted the awesome technology of God to represent phenomena outside the laws of nature.

Starting with the Book of Genesis, we read: "In the beginning God created the heavens and the earth." And our little minds have asked how God could have done this. (The Hebrew word for created, used in the original text, means, literally, "to create out of nothing.")

And since no logical answer is within our comprehension, we have assumed that the illogical alternative must hold the key: that God must have done it all without regard for the laws of nature.

Does this make sense? We make that which is difficult to understand even more incomprehensible by insisting that supernatural powers are responsible. If we were to witness a performer snap his fingers and cause a full-grown elephant to disappear from the stage, wouldn't we be compounding the mystery by suggesting that the illusion was created through the use of supernatural powers? For it matters not whether the performer was man or God; one must still answer the question: How was it done? Where did the elephant go? Is the elephant still alive? Did the sound of the snap of the fingers really cause the elephant to disappear, or did mental power (whatever that is) somehow cause the elephant to disintegrate?

In all, it appears much easier to speculate on the possibilities of the act if we exclude the meaningless word *supernatural*. Then at least we can make some logical determinations, many of which, in the case of the elephant, I am sure have already occurred to the reader.

However, in the case of God creating the heavens and the earth, the problem is a little more staggering; but, as in the case of the elephant, nothing is gained by suggesting that God did it by the use of supernatural power. If Moses had written, "In the beginning God flew from earth to all the planets," then, up to thirty or forty years ago man would have believed that God had a supernatural method of traveling. But, instead, Moses said, "In the beginning God created the heavens and the earth"—which is exactly what He did!

Moses wrote next in Genesis, "The earth was waste and void; darkness covered the abyss, and the spirit of God was stirring above the waters." Today's astronomers and astrophysicists, impaled on the straggling, puny thorns of knowledge cultivated in the past two hundred years or so, struggle with the dilemma of how the earth and all other heavenly bodies came into being. Convinced that some peculiar sequence of natural accidents caused it all, and equally convinced that no conceivable accidents of nature could cause the creation of an object as simple as a fountain pen, they bumble and stumble; and neglect completely the clues God offers in the opening chapters of Genesis. Put simply, scientists, some of whom know God through the word of the Bible, do not believe the Bible.

Unfortunately, those who *do* believe the Bible see, in these opening chapters, evidence that God is supernatural. Not only do they perceive the claims as impossibilities under known laws of nature, but also they read into the clause "the spirit of God was stirring above the waters" that God is a spirit. But look again—no such claim is made. It merely says that the spirit of God was stirring above the waters. If I should claim that the spirit of '76 would once again stir over the United States, would I be claiming that '76 was a spirit?

It is only because we have been staggered and mesmerized by the awesomeness of the claims that we have retreated to the superstitious stance which views it all as having happened through magic; and, as I have stated, those who can't accept magic as the answer have merely shrugged off biblical accounts of happenings as myths and legends. But look what we have if we accept the Bible for what it is: If God did it as He said He did, the Book of Genesis is full of clues that science has completely ignored.

If we assume that the Bible is the word of God, a supertechnological entity and not a spirit, then we can learn much about the manner, method, and sequence of the creation of not only the earth and all thereon, but also of our entire galaxy.

Reading Genesis as a science textbook, we see that the earth did indeed start as a wild, desolate, and dark continuous ocean of water. Today, only a very few astrophysicists give much credence to theories of creation which claim the formation of planets prior to emission of radiation from the sun. But the Bible says it is so. For God said, speaking above the dark watery earth below, "Let there be light," or, as it is sometimes translated, "Let there light be made," (instructions to His angels; not magic words) and there was light.

On the second day (not twenty-four hours, but a more universal period of time—possibly the average time it takes for a galaxy to make a revolution), during that second period of time it appears that an over-abundance of water was on the earth, and that God found it necessary to move or elevate much of this water high off the face of the earth and to leave it suspended somewhere above the atmosphere. For the Book says: "Then God said, 'Let there be a firmament in the midst of the waters to divide the waters.' And so it was. God made the firmament, dividing the waters that were below the firmament from those that were above it. God called the firmament Heaven. And there was evening and morning the second day." (The word *firmament* is taken as meaning "space," for which there is no Hebrew word.)

We can only speculate on the manner in which God performed this feat, for no other clues are given. It would seem plausible, however, even with our limited knowledge of physical science, that large quantities of water could be removed from the surface of the earth and set into orbit awaiting such time as it was needed, and then, by reducing its velocity below orbiting speed, be sent back to earth.

Not only does this explanation fit in nicely with the story of the Flood, but it also accounts for the mistakes made in the carbon-14 dating referred to earlier. For if the earth were cloaked in a canopy of water in those days, then much of the radiocarbon from the sun would have been filtered out; and the result would be that the carbon dating process would indicate ages much greater than they actually were.

It was during the third day that God commanded the angels to separate the waters on the earth so that the dry land would appear. "And so it was." Also during this third day of creation, vegetation was introduced to planet Earth. And I reiterate: No accident of nature can account for the phenomenon of vegetable life, animal life, nor, for that matter, can accidents account for the creation of even a simple atom.

If, as construed by some biblical scholars, God created the sun and the moon on the fourth day, then it becomes difficult to understand how the process of photosynthesis could have sustained vegetation which, I have just pointed out, was put there on the third day. The confusion lies in the following quote: "God made the two great lights, the greater light to rule the day and the smaller one to rule the night, and He made the stars." Since this happened on the fourth day, I propose that the "two great lights" are not the sun and the moon, but rather artificial satellites stationed originally in fixed positions to observe and control the early processes on earth. Admittedly there are poetic phrases in the Bible, but I do not think the phrases "the greater light to *rule* the day" and "the lesser light to *rule* the night" were meant to be poetic; rather, I believe the use of the word *rule* is significant: that two great satellites were originally in position to do just that—to rule! For if, as the evidence seems to indicate, God and His society created the earth as a work of art—so to speak—then it should not come as a surprise that a station for viewing, monitoring, and ruling should have been included in the plans. When the society in Heaven was satisfied that all was in order on earth, and when the population here became too unwieldy to monitor by two fixed stations, then these two great satellites might well have been removed and replaced with smaller, individual vehicles designed to monitor us, the consignees of the guardian angels.

Also, from the same quote in the Bible, we see that the stars were made at this time. The signficance of this fact is tremendous in terms of understanding how galaxies are formed: It appears (since the sun, located near the outer edge of our galaxy, emitted radiation before the stars were visible) that stars nearer the center of spiral galaxies are generally younger, and thus emit radiation later than outer stars such as our own sun. (A new theory on the nature of matter, to be discussed in the last chapter of this book, offers circumstantial evidence supporting this claim of the Bible.)

On the fifth day God stocked the waters of earth with life, and He created the birds of the air. But it wasn't until the sixth day that God completed the scene which He originally contemplated for planet Earth—that is, the creation of animal life, and particularly the creation of man in His (God's) image. Is it not significant that Moses, in writing the story of creation, could (even in 2000 B.C.) know that the elements of living organisms were not chemically unique: the elements of the earth (clay) being no different from the elements of flesh? How could Moses have known that?

Since I have already discussed the merits of spontaneous creation as opposed to evolution, I'll not dwell on the subject further except to speculate on the method God used to create the various kinds of life.

A concept which we all are aware of but to which, perhaps, we have never given conscious recognition accounts for God's ability to create living organisms. That concept tells us that: All that exists *is* and therefore can be duplicated. Those who believe in evolution must admit that even accidents of nature—unplanned and subject to the astronomical odds of probability—did create man. So, with evolutionists, there should be no argument against the possibility that intelligent direction could, in theory, duplicate those accidents of nature. For the spiritists or supernaturalists, however, this concept may fall on deaf ears, for they believe that man is a paradoxical mixture of physical and spiritual being; and that therefore duplication of the physical body would not give us the whole man. (Duplication of the physical body of a plant or animal, however, in the spiritists' eyes might give us the whole, living organism.) To them—the believers by faith—I will only comment that it matters not how one believes God did it, so long as one believes God did it. But for those who demand reason, an exploration of this concept will be enlightening.

Considering the possibilities of reproducing an automobile, no one would deny that others besides the original builders could, from a careful study, build an exact duplicate. The various parts, made from known substances, could be reproduced and placed in the exact relative position as in the original model. The game of reproduction becomes then the art of duplicating the parts and then arranging them according to the original plan.

Regardless of the fact that living organisms are tremendously more complicated than inorganic objects such as cars, the same concept, however, still applies: If the substance of the parts is known then, provided the know-how is present, the parts can be arranged exactly as needed to produce any object—organic or inorganic. God, with complete knowledge of nature's laws, could create a DNA coded cell (having a definite shape and form, as well as a definite composition) and create any life form He so desired.

It is only because man himself has not yet created living organisms that we find it difficult to believe that God has always known how to do it. But, think: As complicated as is a radio, if one but combines the right elements in the right positions and also provides the right conditions, he can create a "living" radio. (The ability to receive electromagnetic signals is, in a sense, analogous to life.) A half century ago, had someone suggested that man could create a machine capable of the mathematical calculations of today's tiny digital computers, he would have been branded an idiot. Perhaps in another half century man will achieve a breakthrough in the field of biochemistry and create an organic computer—a living cell. Steps in this direction have already been taken by way of creation of amino acids (the building blocks of living matter) in a test tube.

New evidence suggests that Adam's mate, Eve, was indeed created from Adam's rib—by a process which is now receiving tremendous interest in the biological laboratories of the world. The process by which an exact duplicate of a parent plant is grown from a single cell of the parent is called "cloning." While to the date of this writing, cloning has only been successfully employed to reproduce plant life, it is nevertheless obvious that we shall eventually find it possible to reproduce animal life by the same process. Some biologists have even expressed the possibility that in order to meet the growing demand for food, it may be possible to clone in such a manner that only the meat of the animal can be grown, without having to create the entire animal.

At any rate, an understanding of the process of cloning diminishes somewhat the mystery of the biblical account of God's creating Eve from the rib of Adam. And in fact, we shall find that the better we understand nature, the less apt we are to disparage any claims made by the authors of the Bible.

It is only by a natural evolution of scientific progress that the masses can be educated. Leapfrogging befuddles the mind. So it is not surprising that twentieth-century man, refusing to accept "supernatural" as an explanation of anything, looks at the claims of the Bible, and not realizing that technology far in advance of that of his own culture is being discussed, simply excludes the possibility that the stories are true.

Continuing in Genesis, we find that Adam and Eve, according to God, "have become like one of us, knowing good and evil." Scholars of the Bible, running the gamut from the absurd to the sublime, have attempted to explain this and other events in the Bible as mythical, symbolic, or even coded messages. I submit that all these conclusions are erroneous. The truth of the matter is just as the Bible claims: Eve experienced an unnatural act involving a serpent and thus learned the concept of lust, which she in turn imparted to Adam. Whenever parables are used in the Bible, no secret is made of the fact, as evidenced by the many explanations of parables made in the New Testament.

God and His society in Heaven may have been displeased with the conduct of Adam and Eve, but there can be little doubt that God could have prevented their sin if He had so desired. In all, it would appear that the evolution of society is generally governed by God's wisdom, and that the condition we find in the world today is much as God planned it from the beginning. For example, we read in Ecclesiasticus* 3:22, "Seek not the things that are too high for thee, and search not into things above thy ability: but the things that God hath commanded thee, think on them always, and in many of His works be not curious." These instructions were violated in the ancient days of the city of Shinar, where was built the Tower of Babel, and mankind threatened to leapfrog God's timetable for the evolution of science. For this, God made them to speak in strange tongues and He scattered them over the face of the earth.

An obscure point in the Book of Genesis concerns the spread of civilization. The specific question is: Where did Adam's offspring find mates? Few clues are given in the Scriptures, but it must be remembered that the Bible is replete with omissions. We can conclude that this condition is intentional; that books of the Bible have not been lost if they are pertinent and that, therefore, information missing from the Bible is missing either because it is not important or because God determined that we should not have it.

In the case of the early propagation of the race of mankind, it is not difficult to perceive that if God could create Adam and Eve, He could also create others—which is exactly what He must have done. However, to explain the differences in the races of humans, we can look to another explanation. In Genesis 6:1, we read, "When man began to multiply on the earth, and had daughters born to them, the sons of God saw that the daughters of man were fair, and they took wives for themselves, as many as they wished. . . . There were giants on the earth in those days and afterward, when the sons of God had relations with the daughters of men who bore children to them."

It would seem difficult indeed to misinterpret this passage from the Bible, notwithstanding the absurd attempts of religious officials to do so by claiming that "the sons of God" refers to good God-fearing descendants of Seth and Enos (Adam's good sons) and that

---

* A Book from The Apocrypha.

"the daughters of men" refers to descendants of Cain (Adam's bad son). It is obvious that such explanations need not be dignified even by refutation. If, indeed, we even consider such distortions of obviously stated facts, there remains little point to reading the Bible, for, under these conditions, we can interpret a simply stated fact to mean the diametric opposite of what it appears to be.

The use of the phrase "sons of God" in this passage makes it clear that the Bible is referring to beings other than earthlings; otherwise, we must conclude that the interbreeding of "good guys" and "bad girls" results in gigantic offspring.

If the original earthlings, Adam and Eve, were pygmies (which there is every reason to believe is true), then the crossbreeding with the beings from other worlds might have produced offspring considerably larger than the pygmy mothers; these would be the "giants" of this passage of the Bible. The occurrence of this incident would also provide an explanation of the origin of the various races of man.

Shortly after this time (if the story in the Bible follows a chronological sequence), God saw that man was evil and so decided to "wipe from the earth man whom I have created—man and beast, crawling creature and bird of the air—for I regret that I made them."

I submit here that, whether man had become evil or not, the Flood would have proceeded, for it was a physical necessity: Earth's water supply was being depleted. We might consider, for example, why God saw fit to vent His anger on all living creatures if it were only man who had become evil.

The truth of the matter is that water vapor, being a gas, is constantly escaping the earth's gravity field. The strange elastic quality of the molecules of gases imparts to them, on collision with one another, velocities in excess of that which is necessary for them to escape earth's gravity; and therefore, as with all gases light enough to reach earth's outer atmosphere, water molecules are lost through this process. If it weren't for the fact that oxygen is constantly being manufactured through photosynthesis, our supply of that vital commodity would eventually be depleted; not only because we use it wastefully but also because we are losing it constantly by the process just described.

There is, however, no indication that water is being manufactured by any similar natural process, and so it appears that we are slowly but steadily losing our supply. As pointed out earlier, God, in creating the earth, overstocked it with water in recognition of the peculiar phenomenon just described. And also, as pointed out earlier, He stored the excess in orbit around the earth, where it remained until the steadily escaping molecules added up and caused a serious depletion. Then, restocking the earth with the stored supply, He caused the great Flood.

We may conclude from the details given in the story of Noe that God took measures to insure that various species would survive the ordeal, but if Noe did indeed follow God's instructions to load the Ark with specific numbers of every living species on earth, then we must conclude that God took a more active part in the "roundup" than the Bible indicates. Through the use of a technological device (which I shall discuss later) God must have caused these creatures to come to Noe. Otherwise, it is inconceivable that Noe could have followed God's instructions as the Bible says he did. (This same device, capable of controlling both the actions and thoughts of living creatures, is apparently one of God's favorite tools; through its use He has caused donkeys to talk, locusts to swarm, hungry lions to remain gentle, and swine to walk off a cliff to a watery death. And, as will be shown, many other miracles of the Bible can be accounted for by this brain-manipulating device.)

One last thought concerning the story of the Flood: God, knowing that the waters stored in orbit were now depleted, made a covenant with Noe. He said, "Never again shall all flesh be destroyed by the waters of the flood; never again shall there be a flood to destroy the earth." Instead, knowing full well that the waters of earth would eventually disappear, God foretold that the earth would be destroyed by fire. The likelihood of fire, as we well know, increases dramatically in areas of drought. Is it any wonder, then, that God predicts the earth will be destroyed by fire?

The rest of the Book of Genesis deals with the geneology of the descendants of Noe, culminating with the story of Joseph, who found favor with the Pharaoh of Egypt and was thus instrumental in bringing the Israelites into Egypt, where they remained for a number of years as a favored people.

CHAPTER 5
Exodus

There is every reason to believe that the enslavement of the Israelites by ·the Egyptians and the subsequent flight to freedom (with the obvious help of God) was, in fact, a programmed episode, the purpose of which was to dramatize the power of God. For just as a parent finds it expedient to exhibit power to his children, whether by the paddle or by the withholding of privileges, so also God recognized the necessity of establishing evidence of His power in order that His children would accept His authority.

The enslavement in Egypt, as students of the Bible are aware, came about as the consequence of the activities of Joseph, who acted in the capacity of God's agent. Through employment of a technological device, the prototype of which man on earth is now in the process of developing, God made it appear that Joseph could read and interpret dreams. (For details of this device, see chapter 7.)

Through the use of this device God made it appear to the Pharao of Egypt that Joseph could correctly interpret his (the Pharao's) dreams. When Joseph correctly interpreted the Pharao's famous dreams of the seven fat and seven lean cows and the seven full and seven scrawny ears of grain, telling Pharao that these two dreams meant that seven good years of harvest would be followed by seven years of famine, the Pharao put Joseph in charge of collecting and storing the grain for the impending shortage and also put him in charge of the distribution of the reserve during the seven years of famine.

So accurate were Joseph's predictions of the circumstances of the episode that, literally, Egypt was saved from starvation. In gratitude, the Pharao offered all the best of the whole land of Egypt to the family of Joseph. And so, from the land of Canaan, Jacob, the father of Joseph, and all his descendants came in glory and luxury to the land of Pharao.

The Book of Exodus opens about four hundred years after the grand entry of the Israelites into Egypt. Joseph and all his brothers are now dead, and a new Pharao is reigning in the land. The new king, who knew nothing of Joseph, said to his subjects, "Look how powerful the Israelite people are growing, more so than we ourselves!" And so the descendants of Jacob were oppressed and placed into slavery.

Shall we assume that God was surprised by this turn of events? On the contrary, for even those who believe God to be supernatural would admit that God knew the Israelites would be thus enslaved, and so the only conclusion we can draw is that God planned the entire episode.

Without the enslavement in Egypt, the history of the Israelites and their obvious affiliation with God would have been considerably less dramatic; for seldom are stories exciting when there is no villain. And there can be no denying that the Egyptians played this role with exceptional vigor: they were cruel, oppressive, stubborn, and even courageous. (Perhaps we shall never know how much of this was natural and how much was enforced by the technology of the stage director.) At any rate, the scene to which Moses was first introduced was ideal for the drama which was to unfold.

Even the circumstances of Moses's birth and subsequent adoption by the Pharao's daughter were expedient to God's plan. For Moses assuredly became more effective as a leader of the Israelites by first having the experience of living in the Egyptian court and becoming intimately acquainted with Egyptian thinking.

Shortly after attaining manhood, Moses visited a forced labor camp and there witnessed an Egyptian taskmaster striking an Israelite slave. Moses became infuriated at this spectacle and proceeded to slay the Egyptian tormentor: This? Even though he himself had been brought up as an Egyptian? Certainly, other Egyptians besides Moses must have witnessed similar acts of brutality; but it is doubtful that any of them ever went to the aid of the tormented.

But the time was right; and, for whatever reason, Moses became enraged, slew the Egyptian, and fled to Midian, where he was "adopted" by an Israelite family. There, as an Israelite, he grew in the knowledge of the plight of his people.

Once this phase of Moses's education was completed, God took a more direct approach and appeared to Moses in a "burning bush"—or, at least, that's what it appeared to be to Moses. But let's investigate this incident more closely. In Exodus 3:2 we read: "There an angel of the Lord appeared to him in fire flaming out of a bush. As he looked on, he was surprised to see that the bush, though on fire, was not consumed." When Moses, out of curiosity, attempted to approach the bush for a better look, God reproached him, demanding that he come no closer. For we read: "God said, 'Come no nearer! Remove the sandals from your feet, for the place where you stand is holy ground. I am the God of your father . . .'" Note: The *angel* of the Lord says, "I am the God of your father . . ." We see from this, as pointed out earlier, that the angel was in such intimate contact with God that he could, in all honesty, speak as God. (Imagine the communications system necessary to validate one's claim of being another: it would require a system at least as elaborate as that between your hand and your head.)

God did not want Moses to approach the "burning bush," not because the ground was holy (He never gave this as a reason, if one reads the narrative carefully) but, rather, because close inspection might have revealed the true nature of the illusion. Or, another possibility is that Moses would have been endangered from radiation. At any rate, no matter what method God used to cause the illusion, we may safely conclude that it was not supernatural; for even with our comparatively primitive technology we could easily create the identical illusion.

God informed Moses, at this time, that he (Moses) would lead his people out of enslavement to the land of "milk and honey." When Moses complained that he was incompetent for the job, God said, "I will be with you . . ." And then God showed Moses various illusions which he could use to prove his affinity with God.

But again Moses pleaded incompetence, saying, "If you please, Lord, I have never been eloquent, neither in the past, nor recently . . . but I am slow of speech and tongue." God's answer to this petition, while seeming trivial, will be seen as tremendously significant when, later, we study the life and miracles of Jesus. In Exodus 4:11, God answered Moses, saying: "Who gives one man speech and makes another deaf and dumb? Or gives sight to one and makes another blind? Is it not I, the Lord?"

But Moses persisted and had his way; God consented to have Moses's brother, Aaron, assist Moses—but God remained adamant in His conviction that He would teach both Moses and Aaron to be eloquent.

In his first attempt at speech, Moses appeared a failure, for when he and Aaron petitioned the Pharao to allow the Israelites three days away from their labor in order that they might go into the desert to pay homage to God, the Pharao reacted negatively and increased the labor of the Israelite slaves. Actually, however, no fault of Moses or Aaron, either in speech or demeanor, caused this turn of events: the infinite wisdom of God (which we can now view in retrospect) fathomed that it would be expedient—if not absolutely necessary—to incite the Israelites to near rebellion if they were to follow Moses on the precarious adventures which lay ahead.

Now, with the Egyptians fiercely tormenting the Israelite slaves, the Israelite foremen badgered Moses to have some action from God. But when Moses asked God for assistance, none was forthcoming: Instead, he was commanded to go once again to the Pharao and demand that the Pharao let his people go. In Exodus

7:1, God says to Moses: "See, I have made you as God to Pharao, and Aaron your brother shall act as your prophet. You shall tell Pharao all that I command you. In turn, your brother Aaron shall tell Pharao to let the Israelites leave his land." And then notice what God says: "Yet I will make Pharao so obstinate that, despite the many signs and wonders that I will work on the land of Egypt, he will not listen to you." Seriously now, how can there be any doubt that God arranged the entire episode? He has revealed in this passage that He was playing both ends against the middle: He was arranging for Moses to make a dramatic exodus from Egypt, and, to insure a suspenseful drama, He promised that He would make the Pharao "obstinate."

And then, in order to demonstrate His power (which demonstration was essential to the plan) God had Moses strike Egypt with the ten famous plagues, culminating with the Passover, which meant death to every firstborn in every Egyptian household. It defies logic to place the responsibility for these deaths on anyone but God; and since most of the victims were not yet out of the cradle, we may safely conclude that God does not consider death of the flesh as punishment for earthly sins. As to the method God used to accomplish this mass execution, we can only conjecture, but a recent study has shown that genetic patterns make some races susceptible to illnesses to which other races are immune. Perhaps in this finding there is a clue.

Concerning Pharao's stubbornness, any ordinary man, acting free of duress, would have capitulated long before he did; but, with God's assistance, he endured every persuasion Moses could inflict—until the Passover, when, apparently, God decided that the demonstration had been sufficient. Then Pharao summoned Moses and told him to take his people and leave the land of Egypt.

The Egyptian people likewise urged the Israelites to leave, believing that otherwise they all would die as had their firstborn. And, attesting to the efficiency of God's plan, the Egyptian people gave to the Israelites whatever they asked in order to hasten them on their way.

To insure that the Israelites would always remember the power of God (and thus obey His laws) He instructed that they should always celebrate the Passover. He commanded them to make that date the first month in their calendar, and He instructed them in the ritual of the ceremony.

When the Israelites left the land of Egypt they took with them much gold and silver and clothing; and also they took "livestock and numerous flocks," but they left in such a hurry that they did not have time to leaven their bread or to prepare foodstuffs. So they baked the unleavened bread, and Moses said, "Only unleavened bread may be eaten during the seven days." And, insuring that the memory of the power of the Lord would never die in the generations of Israel, Moses said to the people, "On this day you shall explain to your son, 'This is because of what the Lord did for me when I came out of Egypt. It shall be as a sign and as a reminder on your forehead; thus the law of the Lord will ever be on your lips, because with a strong hand the Lord brought you out of Egypt.' "

Keeping in mind God's promise to help Moses in what he was to say, it should be obvious that this speech was inspired by God. And we see here positive evidence that the whole purpose of the Exodus was to establish the Lord's authority and thus insure that His laws would be obeyed both at that time and in all the generations which followed. Unfortunately, however, down through the ages, men have become confused, often mistaking ritual for law. Moses's instructions to his people that they should teach the Exodus to their sons was not a law but was taught as a ritual to remind them of the law.

Not satisfied that the lesson was complete, God decided to have the Pharao pursue the Israelites. He instructed Moses to have his people meander in the desert so as to deceive the Pharao into believing that the Israelites were wandering aimlessly. And God said: "Thus will I make the Pharao so obstinate that he will pursue them. Then I will receive glory through Pharao and all his army, and the Egyptians will know I am the

Lord" (Exodus 14:4). Again, it should be noted that God Himself claims responsibility for Pharao's actions; and, as He points out, Pharao's actions will once again serve to demonstrate the awesome power of the Lord. The story of the opening of the Red Sea and the violent destruction of the Pharao's army remains to this day a vivid narrative in the minds of most Western cultures. And the Israelites remain, after years of persecution and torment, irrevocably subservient to the "Law." No parent ever taught his children as forcefully as did God teach His Israelite children.

We read in Exodus 13:21: "The Lord preceded them [the Israelites] in the daytime by means of a column of cloud to show them the way, and at night by means of a column of fire to give them light." Here again, in this narrative, we see claims which believers have long interpreted as being proof that God works outside the laws of nature, and which nonbelievers have used to illustrate that the Bible is a conglomerate of myths. Notwithstanding the fact that presentday technology, by use of a blimp and dry ice, can create the identical illusion described in this passage, no one, to my knowledge, has ever suggested that God performed this "miracle" through technology.

But knowing that we can duplicate the feat should make it easier for us to believe that the account is true. However, it seems doubtful that God ever used devices as primitive as those now available to man; rather, I think the following account of an unidentified flying object seen on September 14, 1954, southwest of Paris, France, describes a device more likely to resemble God's "column of cloud" than a presentday blimp:

> It was about five in the afternoon. Emerging from a thick layer of clouds that looked like a storm coming up, we saw a luminous blue-violet mist, of a regular shape something like a cigar or a carrot. Actually, the object came out of the layer of clouds in an almost horizontal position, slightly tilted toward the ground and pointing forward, like a submerging submarine.
> This luminous cloud appeared rigid. Whenever it moved, its movements had no connection with the

movements of the clouds, and it moved all of a piece, as if it were some gigantic machine surrounded by mist. It came down rather fast from the ceiling of clouds to an altitude which we thought was perhaps a half mile above us. Then it stopped, and the point rose quickly until the object was in a vertical position, where it became motionless.*

This object was seen and reported by hundreds of people from four different villages south of Paris, and I submit that, if it is not the identical device, it is one very similar to the one used by God to lead the Israelites out of Egypt. (Cloud UFOs are commonly reported objects.)

When the Egyptians were bearing down on the Israelites encamped by the Red Sea, God moved the "column of cloud" to the rear, placing it between the camp and the onrushing horde of Egyptians. More than that, God indicated that the cloud was a piloted vehicle, for He said: "The angel of God who had been leading Israel's camp, now moved and went around behind them. The column of cloud also, leaving the front, took up its place behind them so that it came between the camp of the Egyptians and that of Israel" (Exodus 14:19). The phraseology in this account might lead us to believe that the angel of God was not aboard the cloud UFO; and that, I believe, is an intentional ambiguity. If we keep in mind that God was in the act of impressing with His vast and awesome power both the Israelites of that time and all the generations of man to come, then it was desirable for Him to give the impression that the column of cloud was not a piloted vehicle. Piloted vehicles, after all, are not as mystifying as columns of cloud. If an angel of God had indeed accompanied the Israelites on foot, leaving the front of the camp, as the above narrative explains, to place himself between the two camps, then it seems strange that he is mentioned nowhere else in the Book of Exodus. The only conclusion we can draw is that it was no coincidence that both the angel and the column of

---

* From *Anatomy of A Phenomenon* by Jacques Vallee. Chicago: Henry Regnery Co., 1965.

cloud moved to the rear at the same time; for, clearly, the angel was the pilot of the cloud UFO!

It was Moses, and not the angel of God, who lifted his staff at God's command and appeared to cause the Red Sea to divide. Of course, it is no longer believed that Moses's staff had anything to do with the phenomenon; for, had he lost his staff, we know that the incident would have proceeded in much the same way: perhaps, then, he would have been instructed to snap his fingers. At any rate, we see that God had Moses perform a ritual which actually had no connection with the performance of the deed but which, instead, added a touch of theatrics to the episode.

The reader may be surprised to learn that presentday technology is equipped to duplicate (in form, if not in magnitude) this "miracle" of God, for nothing more complicated than static electricity could have been used to hold back the water. Skeptics may satisfy themselves that water, indeed, is subject to the force of static charges simply by running the water from a tap at its thinnest unbroken stream. When a comb which has been run briskly through the hair a few times is brought close to this stream of water, the stream will be diverted from its vertical course.

Many UFOs (including the one seen near Paris) are capable of gathering water vapor and holding it in a mist about themselves, thus giving the craft the appearance of a cloud. And, as I have just pointed out, since static electric charges can affect water, then we might safely conclude that UFOs generate static electric charges.

A strange, intelligently controlled flying object photographed in 1954 by a California county-road inspector shows the object to be about thirty feet above the ground. Directly below this object, a ring of upward-straining earth debris—dust and vegetation—is plainly in evidence; and because the ring of turbulence is no larger in diameter than the craft above (about thirty feet), we can exclude the possibility that the cause is rocket thrust or prop blast. Rather, it appears that a static electric charge is responsible. But when we contemplate the tremendous charge which would be necessary to act over a distance of thirty feet, we then have a clue as to how the waters of the Red Sea might have been separated. The UFO just described was only thirty feet in diameter, but there are numerous reports of UFOs with diameters in excess of nine hundred feet; and, also, cylindrical or cigar-shaped UFOs have been reported which have been estimated to be as much as a mile long.

If these devices can generate static electric fields whose strength is in proportion to their size, then two of these craft could easily have been used by God to hold back the waters of the Red Sea. By submerging two such devices and anchoring them to the bottom, perhaps ten to fifteen yards apart, their charges would have gathered the water about them, forming two mounds of water and leaving a vacated pathway between the two (see figure 1).

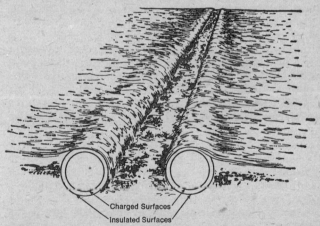

Charged Surfaces
Insulated Surfaces

Figure 1: Cutaway view of the two cylindrical UFOs which could have been used to cause the parting of the Red Sea. The Israelites, fleeing the Egyptians, crossed at night, but in IV Kings (II Kings in King James Bible) we read: "... and fifty men of the sons of the prophets followed them, and stood in sight *at a distance* [italics mine]; but they stood by the Jordan. And Elias took his mantle, and folded it together and struck the waters, and they were divided hither and thither, and they both passed over on dry ground." In daylight would the apparatus pictured above not bear close scrutiny? So it seems!

In the Canticle of Moses, Exodus 15:8, we read: "At a breath of your anger the waters piled up, the flowing waters stood like a mound, the flood waters congealed in the midst of the sea." These lines, from a chant by Miriam, Aaron's sister, indicate clearly that the waters of the Red Sea were piled up, causing the appearance of mounds, just as would be the case if the system just described had been used. It is also, perhaps, significant that the crossing of the sea took place at night, when it would have been impossible to see reflections from the cylindrical vehicles which would have been hidden by only a few feet of water. At daybreak, Moses lifted his staff once more and the waters rushed in to drown the Egyptian charioteers who were in hot pursuit.

Amid all this confusion and with the aid of the semi-darkness of early dawn, the two huge cylinders, lying just below the surface, remained undetected by the Israelite spectators. The Lord had thus executed His plan with the precision we might expect of beings possessing knowledge of all the laws of nature; and, most certainly, there was nothing supernatural about it.

On the wilderness of Sin and during their travels for the next forty years, the Lord, through technology, continued to impress the Israelites with His great power; for not only did He appear to them regularly in His cloud-space vehicle, but He also fed them in the wilderness with a food they called "manna." "It was like coriander seed, but white, and it tasted like wafers made with honey" (Exodus 16:31).

It was only shortly after their crossing of the Red Sea that the children of Israel were "grumbling against the Lord." Then the Lord spoke to Moses and said: "I have heard the grumbling of the Israelites. Tell them: In the evening twilight you shall eat flesh, and in the morning you shall have your fill of bread . . ." (Exodus 16:12).

Fulfilling this promise, the Lord sent quail in the evening to cover the camp; not through supernatural powers but rather through technology which allowed an angel of the Lord to guide the quail to the Israelite camp much as the pilot of a radio-controlled model airplane guides his craft to a desired landing site. Experiments being conducted in several universities today indicate that such control over living creatures is possible: to date, desired responses have been elicited from animals via radio but only after the implantation of electrodes in their brains. However, since these experiments are in their infancy, and since there is also evidence of communications between plants which does not depend on electromagnetic transmissions, it seems more than plausible that we shall one day be able to duplicate this "miracle." Of course, it is altogether possible that by implanting electrodes in the brain of a leader quail, we might—even at this moment—be able to guide a flock to a desired location.

The quail came at twilight, but in the morning, as promised, the sands of the desert were covered with a dew which "evaporated" and revealed fine flakes like hoarfrost on the ground. (If indeed this food was covered with dew, it seems it should have been unpalatably soggy: a much better explanation is that it was covered not with dew but rather with UFO angels' hair, which served to protect it from foraging desert animals.) Moses explained to the people that this was the bread the Lord promised them. And for the remainder of their forty-year stay in the desert, the Lord fed them thusly.

If one chooses to believe that God performed the miracles recorded in Exodus through supernatural powers, then so be it: at least the story is believed. But if in the past one could not accept the narrative simply because the concept of supernatural power seemed absurd, then now at last he has an alternative: now he can believe that God did it all through technology.

And believing the story—supernatural or otherwise—we now see the thrust of God's plan: the young civilization on earth (the infants, so to speak) had to be put in awe of the authority in Heaven. For laws are not obeyed, even by individuals—much less whole societies—unless the lawmaker shows by his actions that he can enforce those laws.

And so, through the enslavement of His "chosen

people" and their subsequent emancipation, God
taught, in the most impressive manner conceivable, the
greatness of His power; His laws have been obeyed
surprisingly well!

From time to time in the remaining books of the Old
Testament God saw fit to reemphasize His power; but,
except for the crumbling of the walls of Jericho (accomplished, in all probability, through the employment
of ultrasonic sound), never does God make such dramatic displays of His power as He did in the events of
Exodus. For example, although the Jordan was opened
similarly to the Red Sea, it is not a commonly known
fact.

It should be obvious then that the reason or reasons
for the remainder of the Old Testament writings were
not to impress mankind with God's power, rather after
the Exodus it remained for God to organize His new
society. In the Book of Leviticus, God outlines the
hierarchy of the ministry, assigning to the house of Levi
the responsibility for propagating and strengthening
divine worship. And He outlined the rules for legal
purity, the rules for sacrifices, and rules for other acts
designed to remind the whole house of Israel to obey
the laws. (The distinction should be clearly drawn: the
rules of the ministry are not the moral laws. The moral
laws are the last seven of the Ten Commandments,
which pertain specifically to man's treatment of man.)

The Books of Numbers and Deuteronomy also are
concerned with rules for the young Israelite society. But
it is obvious that those rules, given at that time, were
not meant to be enforced forever, but instead were
meant to apply only during that era when they were
relevant. As pointed out earlier, we make the rule for
a young child not to climb the stairs, but we certainly
don't expect the child to obey this rule forever. And so
God (viewing society as we view a child) gave rules
which would protect and organize His young society.

The books which follow in the Old Testament serve
primarily as a diary to preserve in exact detail the history of God's chosen people. Occasionally, however, a
book of the Old Testament will serve to teach a lesson.

The Book of Baruch,* the Book of Ruth, and of course the Book of Job are examples of God's moral teachings.

Finally, among the books of the Old Testament are the Books of the Prophets which serve the dual purpose of keeping man in awe of the "mysteries" of God and reinforcing the impact of the Father image, Jesus, the Christ.

---

* A Book from The Apocrypha.

CHAPTER 6
Jesus, the Father Image

"Amen Amen I say to you, the son can do nothing of himself, but only what he sees the father doing"

(John 5:19).

As His society on earth began to mature, God, as He had planned from the beginning, presented mankind with father images. (Remember, there were others besides Jesus.) These images were to be perfect models after which God's children should seek to fashion moral and ethical behavior.

To insure that Jesus would be accepted as His agent, God foretold His coming. Abraham is told that he will have a descendant who would be a blessing to all the people of the earth (Genesis 12:1–3). And the prophet Micheas, writing nearly a thousand years before the event, says, "And thou, Bethlehem Ephrata, art a little one among the thousands of Juda: out of thee shall he come forth unto me that is to be the ruler of Israel: and his going forth is from the beginning from the days of eternity" (Micheas 5:2).

Isaias foretold the "miracles" Jesus would perform. Speaking of the coming Messiah, the prophet says, "He will come and save you. Then the eyes of the blind shall be opened, and the ears of the deaf unstopped: then shall the lame man leap like a hart, and the tongue of the dumb sing for joy" (Isaias 35:4–6). Those who claim that such prophecies were written after the fact might be surprised to learn that a complete Book of Isaias was among the recent Dead Sea Scroll findings. And it has been definitely established that these writings date back at least to 100 B.C.

In Psalm 22, written by David (in whose lineage Jesus was born as prophesied by Nathan), we read a description of Christ's ordeal by crucifixion—which form of execution was not even known at the time David wrote the psalm. He does not name the form of the execution, yet he describes the circumstances in such detail (a thousand years before the event) that there can be little argument but that he was describing Jesus's agony on the cross.

He writes, "My God, my God, why have you forsaken me, far from my prayer, from the words of my cry." (Notice, the opening words of this psalm were used by Jesus on the cross; and of course it might be claimed that Jesus, being familiar with this passage, simply used it for emphasis. However, that still does not explain how David could have written the whole thing a thousand years before.) The psalm continues: "O my God, I cry out by day, and you answer not: by night, and there is no relief for me." (Then note well the next line, for it is crucial to the point of this book—that God is physical.) "Yet you are enthroned in the holy place." (Where you can hear me and answer my prayers?) "O glory of Israel!"

"In you our fathers trusted; they trusted, and you delivered them.

"To you they cried, and they escaped; in you they trusted, and they were not put to shame.

"But I am a worm, not a man; the scorn of men, despised by the people.

"All who see me scoff at me; they mock me with parted lips, they wag their heads:

" 'He relied on the Lord; let him deliver him, let him rescue him, if he loves him.'

"You have been my guide since I was first formed, my security at my mother's breast.

"To you I was committed at birth, From my mother's womb you are my God."

Verse 2

"Be not far from me, for I am in distress; be near, for I have no one to help me.

"Many bullocks surround me; the strong bulls of Bashan encircle me.

"They open their mouths against me like ravening and roaring lions.

"I am like water poured out; all my bones are racked.

"My heart has become like wax melting away within my bosom.

"My throat is dried up like baked clay, my tongue cleaves to my jaws; to the dust of death you have brought me down.

"Indeed, many dogs surround me, a pack of evildoers closes in upon me." (Interestingly, during the time of Jesus, gentiles were often referred to as "dogs.")

"They have pierced my hands and my feet; I can count all my bones.

"They look on and gloat over me; they divide my garments among them, and for my vesture they cast lots."

Anyone familiar with the details of the Crucifixion will recognize the amazing accuracy of this prophecy. With all of this, it is hard to understand why Jesus was not accepted by His own people, the Jews. But it must be remembered that, while the Jews were looking for a promised Messiah, they were not expecting a suffering Messiah. Rather, they were looking for a dramatic and powerful Savior who would deliver them from their oppressors. And so, at least for those who were looking for a conquering hero, Jesus was not accepted.

It remained for the gentiles (who actually were not even looking for a messiah) to finally accept Jesus as an agent of God. And it was primarily through the work of the apostles that the good news was spread. For it was the apostles who traveled throughout the area of the Mediterranean telling of Jesus, His teachings and His "miracles." Today, most of the Western world reveres Jesus as the true Savior and the model after which their societies should try to fashion their lives. Jesus is their father image!

How did God accomplish this? How did He cause Jesus to be accepted as the father image? For even those who believe the story of Jesus to be fraudulent must, nevertheless, admit that the sheer numbers of His followers are unprecedented. And it might be all the more impressive should we learn that Jesus never did exist.

As we have seen, God utilized the power of prophecy to help Jesus gain recognition, but His efforts did not end there; for, as well as being introduced to mankind through prophecy, Jesus was also involved and assisted by the perfect technology of God and His heavenly hosts.

To begin with, we are told that Jesus was born of a virgin—which story in the past meant a supernatural birth. But today, in the Age of Reason, we can look for a different explanation. Examining the alternatives, we find we have three choices: we can claim that the story is a myth—either a contrived lie or the culmination, perhaps, of a series of exaggerations. This explanation, I believe, is more respectable than that which has been accepted by the believers for the past two thousand years—that is, that God did it supernaturally. And finally, the third possibility is that God did exactly as the Bible says He did. We read, according to Luke 1:26–35, "Now in the sixth month the angel Gabriel was sent from God to a town of Galilee called Nazareth, to a virgin betrothed to a man named Joseph, of the house of David, and the virgin's name was Mary. And when the angel had come to her, he said, 'Hail, full of grace, the Lord is with thee. Blessed art thou among women.' When she had heard him she was troubled at his work, and kept pondering what manner of greeting this might be.

"And the angel said to her, 'Do not be afraid, Mary, for thou hast found grace with God. Behold, thou shalt conceive in thy womb and shalt bring forth a son; and thou shalt call his name Jesus. He shall be great, and shall be called the Son of the Most High; and the Lord God will give him the throne of David his father, and he shall be king over the house of Jacob forever; and of his kingdom there shall be no end.'

"But Mary said to the angel, 'How shall this happen, since I do not know man?'

" And the angel answered and said to her, 'The Holy

Spirit shall come upon thee and the power of the Most High shall overshadow thee; and therefore the Holy One to be born shall be called the Son of God. And behold, Elizabeth thy kinswoman also has conceived a son in her old age, and she who was called barren is now in her sixth month; for nothing shall be impossible with God.' "

It will be noted that the particular angel, Gabriel, was sent to a particular town (suggesting that he had to travel to get there; thus obeying at least one natural physical law). And the angel spoke to her and she heard. (Again we see the angel subject to natural law.) And note, when Mary asked how she would conceive, Gabriel did not say it would be done supernaturally; instead he said the Holy Spirit (which, as the evidence I will shortly present indicates, is a technological communications device with the facility to induce hypnosis) would come upon her. In other words, she would be anesthetized by hypnosis, and then she would be "overshadowed" (what better word could describe her condition) by the power of the Most High. If we accept a reasonable explanation of what is being said here, it is obvious that Mary is being told that, without submitting to any man and while not being aware of what was happening, she would be impregnated.

At the time Luke wrote this narrative, the idea that Mary could have been impregnated artifically would have seemed more absurd than the idea that she could conceive supernaturally. But today, artifical insemination is a common occurrence and nothing to inspire awe. In the case of Mary, however, we know that pains were taken to insure that her hymen would remain intact; otherwise, the midwives at Jesus's birth would not know that Mary was a virgin; thus, we may conclude that her insemination was accomplished with a hypodermic needle.

And so we see, the biblical account never claims that God acted outside the laws of cause and effect, but still, the appearance of awesome, mystical powers was inherent in the act. It should be obvious that God's intent was to present mankind with a father image whose birth was a mysterious event. For, after all, how could the offspring of a mere human serve as the father image for nearly half the population of the earth?

Perhaps if the prophecies and the virgin birth were the only miracles associated with Jesus, He might still be remembered for His profound teachings, but certainly He would not have the following He has today. God saw to it that Jesus would be remembered not only for His wisdom and miraculous birth, but also because of the Resurrection and because of the countless miraculous healings which He performed.

If anyone believes that Jesus truly healed without regard for the laws of cause and effect, then how does He explain the details of the cures? For example, if Jesus causes sightless eyes to see, what physical changes take place in the affected organs when they are corrected? Since, as we know, there can be many causes for blindness, shall we assume that faith healers use the same mystical portent to cure all forms of blindness? Would they exert the same "powers" to cure a man with glaucoma as they would to cure a man with cataracts? And after they exerted this "power," would the cataracts disappear? And if they disappeared, where would they go?

Reason demands answers to these questions: If an organ, incapacitated for any reason, is restored to operable condition, then whether or not we know how it was done, we should, nevertheless, know what changes restored it. In the case of the cataracts, we should know if the growth was removed or if it remained but somehow became transparent. And once we know the answer to that question, we can ask more: What was used to remove the cataracts? Or, what caused them to become transparent? Once we start thinking along these lines, it becomes apparent how absurd it is to ascribe supernatural causes to the cures.

If there were such a thing as supernatural faith healing, then also we should expect healers who could repair mechanical devices in the same manner. For example, picture, if you will, Jesus placing His hand on the hood of a car for the purpose of effecting a "cure."

Let's assume that the car had been gutted by fire—the battery and wiring having been completely destroyed. If Jesus should, by the mere laying on of hands, cause this car to start and run again, many mechanics would want to look under the hood! Common sense tells us that under the hood would be found a new battery and new wiring; otherwise, the car simply would not run. And we would then know that Jesus had used either trickery or technology or both to restore the car.

At any rate, if the car did not operate before and now does, reason tells us that a physical change was made in the car, and physical changes (following the law of cause and effect) are not supernatural. But when organic motors (living organisms) are not running properly, we may (because we don't have a complete understanding of the mechanics) conclude that mystical malfunctions are the cause.

Moreover, concerning Jesus's miraculous cures, Jesus Himself denies time and again that miracles are involved. From Matthew 9:23 we read: "And when Jesus came to the ruler's house, and saw the flute players and the crowd making a din, He said, 'Begone, the girl is asleep, not dead.' And they laughed Him to scorn." A moment later Jesus took the girl by the hand and she awoke. And so we ask: Was this a supernatural event? Christians will claim it was, even though Christ Himself denies it.

Many of Jesus's miracles involved what He referred to as the casting out of evil spirits, and often, according to the biblical accounts, the spirits would speak, and be heard not only by Jesus but also by all those present.

Despite our recent preoccupation with belief in "possession" by evil spirits, it is absolutely absurd to think that such things as evil spirits exist. I will show that the evil spirits which Jesus cast out were not supernatural and that they were not anything at all like the things we have perceived them to be. There simply cannot be such a thing as unphysical spirit beings. If there were, there could be no way by which we could perceive them, and there could be no way in which they could interact with physical beings.

Perhaps the best way to explain the fallacy of the concept that physical beings can be influenced by spirit beings is to make the analogy once again with the inorganic machine, the atomobile. Certainly, if a spirit being can cause an organic machine to malfunction, then it should have no trouble causing an automobile to break down. So, what does the spirit do to our car? Does it crush the gas line? Does it tear out the wiring? Does it water the gas? If these questions sound ridiculous (and I hope they do, because they *are*) then wouldn't or shouldn't they sound equally as ridiculous when applied to organic machines?

It is only because we don't understand the mechanics of the organic machine that we allow even the possibility of "possession" to enter our minds. But if we remember that we are physical, then we know that nonphysical beings, even if there were such things, cannot cause us to malfunction.

So then, what about the evil spirits of Jesus? If it is true that there are no such things as spirit beings, what then did Jesus mean when He said: "But if I cast out devils by the spirit of God, then the kingdom of God has come upon you" (Matthew 12:28)? Before answering this question, I would like first to analyze biblical references to spirits, demons, devils, and in particular Satan; and determine once and for all just what the authors of the Bible are telling us.

In Job 1:6 we read: "Now on a certain day when the sons of God came to stand [Do spirits stand?] before the Lord, Satan also was among them." If we are to believe this account—which we must, if we believe the Bible to be the Word of God— then we see that Satan is the son of God. And, in fact, on this particular occasion it appears that the meeting was called primarily for God's instructions to Satan. And, furthermore, we see that Satan takes his orders from God: "And the Lord said to Satan: Behold he [Job] is in thy hand, but yet save his life" (Job 2:6).

In fact, whenever we read of Satan in the Scriptures, it never appears that he is acting independently but rather that he is either carrying out God's instructions or that his acts are sanctioned by God. And of course, if we believe God to be all-powerful, then we simply cannot deny that Satan's activities are permitted and thus condoned by God.

Despite the fact that Jesus reviles Satan as a liar and murderer, nevertheless it is obvious that Satan is in the employ of God. In essence, he is the executioner. He is the perpetrator of all the activities which God deems necessary for our social evolution but which would detract from our appraisal of God should we ever suspect that He Himself were committing these acts.

The kindly gentleman who owns a department store retains the image of being nonviolent and even merciful while protecting his customers from higher prices by protecting his store from robbers by using vicious watchdogs. Someone must do the dirty work. And if the store owner refers to the dogs as "vicious," "treacherous," or "bloodthirsty," he is being honest. And yet the dogs are doing his work!

And so it is with Satan: he does God's dirty work. In I Kings 16:14 we read: "But the spirit of God departed from Saul, and an evil spirit from the Lord troubled him." Note: here God admits the employment of evil spirits. Also, from Luke 13:11, "And behold there was a woman who for eighteen years had had a sickness caused by a spirit; and she was bent over and utterly unable to look upwards. When Jesus saw her, He called her to Him and said to her, 'Woman thou art delivered from thy infirmity.'" Who was the culprit that made this woman a cripple for eighteen years so that Jesus could be glorified for curing her? In Jesus's words, we read (Luke 13:16): "And this woman, daughter of Abraham as she is, whom Satan has bound lo, for eighteen years . . ."

The concept that Satan is an agent of God may at first seem heretical, but the evidence shows that the concept is in complete accord with Scripture. Once again, in Jesus's own words: "The Prince of the world [common designation of Satan] is coming, and in me he has nothing. [We do not do the same work.] But he comes that the world may know that I love the Father, and that I do what the Father has commanded me" (John 14:30). Jesus, therefore, testifies that Satan's work will serve to show that He (Jesus) is from God. Why should Satan do that for God and Jesus if he is opposed to them? The answer is obvious: If Satan worked for God in cooperation with Jesus, it is futile to try to explain him as anything but an agent of God.

Equally as futile would be any attempts to substantiate the conclusion that Satan or evil spirits enter a physical body. For while Satan is real and physical, an evil spirit is merely the terminology used by the authors of Scripture to describe what we know today as a hypnotic trance.

To claim that a body is possessed while, in fact, it is under the influence of hypnosis is not altogether untruthful. And the Bible is never untruthful. Presentday knowledge of hypnosis must be considered primitive by agents of God's society, but we know enough at least to understand that somehow the subconscious workings of our bodies can be made to control our conscious activities. All manner of psychosomatic illnesses plague a large segment of society. These are illnesses incurred by the interference of the subconscious with normal functions, usually brought on by trauma in early childhood.

A popular family medical guide says that literally hundreds of symptoms can occur as a result of emotional distress, but these symptoms, it says, are not imaginary, as with hypochondriacs: "They are real and visible, but their origin is emotional rather than physical."* Therein lies the fallacy of the concept; the ulcer in the psychosomatic patient's stomach, according to medical science, while it is itself physical, got there by nonphysical (emotional) causes.

Evidence is slowly but steadily accumulating which indicates that an emotionally disturbed individual is also a chemically (and thus, physically) disturbed individual. Common sense should have made this clear hundreds of years ago. But obviously when things which

---

* *Better Homes and Gardens Family Medical Guide.* Des Moines: Meredith Corporation, 1964.

are not understood are classified "magical" or "super-natural," no other explanation seems necessary. No machine—organic or inorganic—malfunctions without a physical cause. The fact that the cause is not known does not justify our labeling it magical, supernatural, or emotional. Emotions or feelings do, however, signal certain glands which regulate body chemistry, and so, in a manner of speaking, emotions, acting as switches, can trigger physical malfunctions.

The malfunctions which God caused through His agent, Satan, were not, however, strictly in the category of psychosomatic; they were not caused by trauma in the sense in which we know it, but rather by trauma which appears to have been produced by a brain-manipulating device. The evidence indicates that through this device (referred to as the Holy Spirit or simply "spirit" by authors of the Bible), God or Satan could communicate both with the conscious and the subconscious nervous systems of organic beings.

If this explanation of the Holy Spirit (no reason for capitalization) or spirit seems heretical or even impossible scientifically, then consider the following quotations from the Bible in which I have substituted for "spirit" or "holy spirit" the word *telepather* (which can mean either the device itself, or the operator).

Then Jesus was led into the desert by the telepather (Matthew 4:1).

For it is not you who are speaking, but the telepather of your Father who speaks through you (Matthew 10:20) . . . and it was revealed to him by the telepather (Luke 2:25).

Brethren, the Scripture must be fulfilled which the telepather declared before by the mouth of David concerning Judas (Acts of the Apostles 1:16).

And they were all filled with the telepather and began to speak in foreign tongues, even as the telepather prompted them to speak (Acts of the Apostles 2:4).

Stiff necked and uncircumcised in heart and ear, you always oppose the telepather; as your fathers did, so you do also (Acts of the Apostles 8:51). If the reader cares to understand this admonition, read Job 33.

These things I have spoken to you while dwelling with you. But the Advocate, the telepather, whom the Father will send in my name, he will teach you all things, and bring to your mind whatever I have said to you (John 14:17).

From John 14:17, Jesus, speaking of the Advocate, says, "But you shall know him, because he will dwell with you and be in you."

Behold I will send a telepather upon him and he shall hear a message (Isaias 37:7).

He created in them (men) the science of the telepather (Ecclesiasticus* 17:6).

The prophet Zacharias speaks time and again of an angel which speaks not to him but "in" him.

For those who are skeptical about the possibility that such a device as the telepather is scientifically feasible, let me assure you that investigations being conducted today seem to point unerringly to a system of biochemical communication between living cells, both animal and vegetable. And in fact, there is evidence that even elements of the electromagnetic spectrum may be able to effect the autonomic (subconscious) nervous systems of living creatures.

After spending much time and money on the project, the government of the United States has concluded that radar, microwaves, and high-powered radio-transmission waves do affect the nervous system and also alter behavior. As of this writing, it has not been determined how to affect specific behavior, but it would seem safe to assume that it will be done on earth as it has obviously already been done in Heaven.

When the heavenly telepather speaks to the conscious, the contactee receives the message as audible sound, but I believe the communication bypasses the auditory system and directly stimulates the auditory interpreters of the brain. On the other hand, when the communicator signals the subconscious, it appears that almost any type of behavior can be elicited from the contactee, making it appear, for example, that he is

---

* A Book from The Apocrypha.

blind, deaf, mute, insane (possessed), crippled, or even
dead (dead by inducing a state of suspended animation
similar to hibernation).

Also, through this device, it appears that contactees
can be made to see lights and objects much as they
would in a hallucination. Saul, on his way to Damascus
with a group of fellow Christian persecutors, was
blinded by a glaring light which appeared above the
road but only to him, but the voice accompanying the
light was heard also by his companions. It was at this
moment that Saul was converted and later became
known as Paul.

Truly remarkable (and also, perhaps, one of the chief
stumbling blocks to wide acceptance of biblical authenticity) is the tale of Balaam, a soothsayer of the plains
of Moab. Here the Israelites were occupying the land
prior to crossing the Jordan and storming the walls of
Jericho. The telepather was used in this episode to
make it appear that an animal could talk. From Numbers 22:28 we read: "But now the Lord opened the
mouth of the ass and she asked Balaam, 'What have I
done that you should beat me these three times?' " The
animal had balked, having seen a vision of an angel in
the road ahead (obviously by way of the telepather),
and Balaam, not seeing the vision, beat the animal in
the mistaken belief that she was balking out of obsti-
nance. The narrative continues: "Then the Lord removed
the veil from Balaam's eyes so that he too saw the angel
of the Lord standing in the road with sword drawn."

Logically, we may conclude there was no physical
veil over Balaam's eyes; what had to have happened
was, as I have explained: a vision-projecting device was
first used to make the ass think she saw a figure on the
road, and then Balaam himself was subjected to the
device.

This instrument, which can project visions and hallucinations into the minds of men and animals and
which can hypnotize them by sending messages to their
autonomic nervous systems, is one of God's most useful
tools. Stories of its use abound in the Bible, but perhaps

nowhere was it used more extensively than in the life and times of Jesus.

As explained previously, Satan obviously set the stage for Jesus. Through use of the telepather, he caused psychosomatic blindness, deafness, and other disorders; he caused many to be mute, and many to be "possessed." He caused many to be crippled, and he even caused some to be hemophiliacs (bleeders). Coagulation of blood is controlled by the autonomic nervous system. Also, Satan made it appear that certain members of Christ's society were dead. And, as already pointed out, Satan did all this for the specific purpose of glorifying Jesus. For without the cripples of Satan, Jesus could not have performed his miraculous cures.

A careful reading of the Gospels makes it impressively clear that the proposals I make here are true. For example, in the cases involving Jesus's restoring life to the dead: Jesus himself usually states that the bodies are asleep and not dead.

Even Lazarus, who supposedly was dead for four days, was not, according to Jesus, truly dead. In fact, it is clearly stated in John 11:4 that Lazarus is not dead, and furthermore, that it is not intended that he should die, for Jesus says, "This sickness is not unto death, but for the glory of God, that through it the son of God may be glorified." Later Jesus says, "Lazarus, our friend, sleeps. But I go that I may wake him." If he were really only sleeping, we might ask why others besides Jesus could not awaken him.

The mistaken notion that Lazarus was dead comes from a later statement made by Jesus in which it appears that He is stating a fact: "Lazarus is dead," He says. But the text of the narrative indicates that He was merely mouthing the words in contemplation. Lazarus could not be both asleep and dead. Furthermore, if Lazarus had lain a corpse for four days, his body would have been irreparably damaged, and to resurrect him would have required much more attention and repairing than Jesus administered when He said, "Lazarus, come forth!" A further complication in this episode is that

Jesus, knowing He is going to resurrect Lazarus, nevertheless weeps at the burial site. Isn't this somewhat incongruous? Apparently Jesus saw fit to emphasize by this display of emotion that Lazarus was lost. If not that, then perhaps out of compassion for those who really suffered in the mistaken belief that a loved one was dead. Jesus also was moved to tears.

Another similar case is found in Luke 8:52. Jesus says of Jairus's daughter, who is said to be dead, "Do not weep; she is asleep, not dead." Hearing this, those gathered at the place ridiculed Jesus, but Jesus said to the girl, "Girl, arise!" Whereupon she did, and they were amazed. As He often did, Jesus charged the girl's parents to tell no one of this miraculous healing.

And once again common sense tells us that Jesus never expected these events to remain secret. Furthermore, why, if the girl was only sleeping, did He not want anyone to know He had awakened her? The truth of the matter is, Jesus was employing a profound psychological ruse: By appearing to want the event kept secret, He succeeded in magnifying its importance.

Notice also that Jesus's cure of Lazarus was very similar to the cure of the girl: in both instances a simple command such as would be used to bring a subject out of a hypnotic trance was used. Analyzed from the point of view that the word *supernatural* is meaningless, the cases of Jesus casting out devils become easy to accept when we realize that hypnotism was used. And no longer must skeptics preserve their intellectual self-respect by denying the stories (while often wishing to believe in Jesus).

If one does not believe that Jesus cast out devils, then one believes that either Jesus or the Gospel writers were liars, or, worse yet, that Jesus was a deluded religious fanatic. But I assure you He was neither a liar nor a nut: He did as He said He did, freeing the subconscious of those afflicted by Satan's hypnotizing device.

In the story from Mark 5:1, it is so clearly demonstrated that possession by unclean spirits or Satan is, as I have claimed, the result of hypnotism, that it should convince even those who believe by faith. Jesus and the disciples had just arrived in the country of the Gerasenes when they were met by a man possessed, and we read: "And when he saw Jesus from afar, he ran and worshiped him, and crying out with a loud voice, he said, 'What have I to do with thee, Jesus, Son of the most high God? I adjure thee by God, do not torment me!' [These are the words of one of the spirits allegedly in possession of the man.] For Jesus was saying to him, 'Go out of the man, thou unclean spirit.' And Jesus asked him, 'What is thy name?' And he said to him, 'My name is Legion, for we are many.' And he entreated him earnestly not to drive them out of the country. [Remember, this is the voice of the spokesman of the possessing spirits. I wonder what country they expected Jesus might send them to?] Now a great herd of swine was there on the mountain-side, feeding. And the spirit kept entreating him, saying, 'Send us into the swine, that we may enter into them.' And Jesus immediately gave them leave. And the unclean spirits came out and entered into the swine; and the herd, in number about two thousand, rushed down with great violence into the sea, and were drowned in the sea."

Seriously now, can twentieth-century man accept the possibility that invisible, nonmaterial (made of nothing) spirit beings possessed this man? And if they did, we should ask how they got to him, for they have indicated that they cannot get to the swine unless Jesus gives them permission. If they cannot move of their own accord, then who moved them from their original site into the body of Legion? Another revealing question: Since we have seen that the spirits moved from the man to the swine (thus changing locations), what was their location in Legion? (It must have been very crowded in there!) Does it not seem incongruous that that which admittedly has no dimensions (spirits) can occupy specific areas? And finally, we might ask what criteria Satan used to determine that this man of Gerasa needed two thousand evil spirits while, in all other cases, individuals are possessed by only one spirit.

Indeed, it is much more reasonable to surmise that

this man was in a hypnotic trance, and that Satan, in order to dramatize the incident, used the telepather to cause the swine (obviously against their will) to walk over a cliff into the sea. It certainly would have been much more humane to have transferred all two thousand evil spirits into one animal (perhaps animals don't have the capacity of humans) and have just that one commit suicide. But obviously this would not have had the same impact; neither would it have constituted visual proof of the multiplicity of evil spirits. And, of course, had only one swine died, the swineherds would not have made a clamor over the incident.

The first reaction of the reader—when it suddenly becomes clear that Jesus cured by the method described here—may be similar to mine: My first thought when I realized that God had created cripples for the purpose of glorifying Jesus was that God must be cruel and unfeeling. But careful study of the Scriptures reveals that those who suffered as flesh at the hands of Satan and for the benefit of Jesus were to be compensated in the hereafter for their suffering. A key statement supporting this idea came from Jesus Himself, as we have already seen in the quote from Matthew 12:28: "But if I cast out devils by the spirit of God, then the kingdom of God has come upon you."

It appears, then, that those who suffered on behalf of God shall be in the kingdom of God, which, we have been told, is the hereafter in Heaven. And, as pointed out earlier, circumstantial evidence overwhelmingly indicates that reward and punishment for our deeds on earth come not in this life but in an existence apart from our fleshly bodies (see next chapter).

Evidence that technology other than the brain manipulator or telepather were used in behalf of Jesus abounds in the Bible: the feeding of five thousand from five loaves of bread, the water-walking episode, and the calming of a storm were all "miracles" accomplished by a technology which we can only now begin to comprehend.

In the feeding of five thousand, as told in Mark 6, Jesus instructs the people to lie down in groups of fifty and one hundred. Certainly, these are not magic numbers, but obviously, dispositions of people in these amounts would expedite the count being done from the cloud UFO hovering above.

The water-walking episode was also obviously accomplished through use of technology: a UFO concealed in the overcast of either a natural storm or one of its (the UFO's) own creation exerted a static electric charge, the strength of which was regulated by a sonar-type sensor-strength of field, diminishing automatically when Christ's body started to rise and increasing when He started to sink. Such a device could be constructed today even with our limited knowledge of static electric charges.

The question of how Jesus could quell a storm by a command is simplified once we understand that UFOs can cause strange winds to blow. (This from current observations, from observations at the miracle of Fatima, and also from the UFOs in the Bible which are often referred to as "whirlwinds.")

Jesus's well-authenticated ability to read minds can be explained in terms of the telepather: the advocate or telepather would read the mind of the subject and relay the message to Jesus.

Jesus's ability to advise the fishermen where to drop their nets can be explained in terms similar to those explaining the flocks of quail on the desert of Sin: simply speaking, the fish were directed by the telepather.

But perhaps the most dramatic of all the miracles of Jesus and the one for which He is best remembered is the Resurrection. Since Jesus promised eternal life to His followers, it was only fitting that He appear to be the Master of Death. Symbolically, He was saying to us, "See, death cannot hold me, neither can it hold you if you follow me." But Jesus never died that day on the cross at Calvary!

Clinical death, even in this day, is difficult to define. Certain tissues and organs of the body cease to function, not simultaneously, but a little at a time. If Jesus was, as the faithful believe, supernatural, and if He died as they also believe, then how do they explain or define death? Can supernatural beings die? And, furthermore, would a supernatural being allow himself to really die when (as the faithful would readily admit) he would have it well within his power to feign death? Or perhaps he allowed only a small part of himself to die—perhaps only a few cells.

So no matter how we view Jesus—supernatural or supertechnological—there seems no escape from the conclusion that he did not die on the cross. (An intriguing curiosity is that not one of the four Gospel writers says point-blank that Jesus died on the cross. Check it yourself.)

Not only did Jesus not die on the cross, but there seems little reason to suppose that He suffered as much as others who were crucified at the time. Resorting to reason and putting ourselves in God's place, would we really want Jesus (our confederate) to suffer outrageously? Would we, if we could, limit His suffering to an absolute minimum? The answer is obvious: Jesus's suffering on the cross was minimal but sufficient. As a matter of fact, Jesus may have suffered somewhat more than He had anticipated, for I believe it to be rather obvious that Jesus was anesthetized hynotically by the telepather. And the fact that He was a victim of a slight deception is apparent: the Advocate, operating the telepather, was aware of Jesus's feelings, particularly the physical suffering, and yet allowed the suffering to reach proportions which prompted Jesus to cry out the words of the Psalm of David: "My God, my God, why has thou forsaken me?"

We can now answer Jesus's question because, in retrospect, we see that He had to suffer in order to be honest. Since, as the father image, He had to prove His great love for us, and could not have done so without some suffering, the Advocate knew (even as he did back in the time of David) that Jesus had to suffer more than He (Jesus) had anticipated.

Jesus's resurrection was anticlimatic: the real drama and the strength of our faith is embodied in our reverence for the cross. It is the suffering of Jesus which moves us to enshrine His teachings; His resurrection only increased our awe. But, viewed from a rational point of view, Jesus gave us an example to follow: He was the embodiment of love and understanding, a man hand-picked by God to focus our attention on the wisdom of morality and the joy of giving. Truly, a man who fashions his life after Jesus must be justified.

"Be ye therefore imitators of God, as very dear children and walk in love, as Christ also loved us" (Ephesians 5).

CHAPTER 7
And Now Reason

The code of conduct prescribed for man by God through the "Law" and through "Faith" in the various father images is valid only to those who admit that others besides themselves have a right to happiness. An airplane hijacker, holding fifty horrified hostages for the purpose of forcing acceptance of his demands for personal gain, sees little validity in the admonition "Do unto others as you would have them do unto you."

Likewise, the homosexual sees no reason to heed the advice given in II Corinthians 6:9–10: "Do not err; neither fornicators, nor idolaters, nor adulterers, nor the effeminate, nor sodomites, nor thieves, nor the covetous, nor drunkards, nor the evil-tongues, nor the greedy will possess the kingdom of God."

As strange as it may seem, the arguments supporting the logic of God's laws have never been convincing. And, in fact, we find today's society moving farther and farther from the teachings of God. "Act according to your conscience," is the most popular current philosophy. But this bit of reasoning presumes that man is wiser than his creator; and so, based on his own reasoning, man see no particular necessity for obeying scriptural law.

To date, the only reason we have for living according to God's laws is the promise of a mysterious recompense in a life after death. Jesus made this promise with the opening paragraph of His Sermon on the Mount: "Blessed are the poor in spirit, for theirs is the kingdom of heaven. Blessed are the meek, for they shall possess the earth. Blessed are they who mourn, for they shall be comforted. Blessed are they who hunger and thirst for justice, for they shall be satisfied. Blessed are the merciful, for they shall obtain mercy. Blessed are the clean of heart, for they shall see God. Blessed are the peacemakers, for they shall be called children of God. Blessed are they who suffer persecution for justice's sake, for theirs is the kingdom of heaven. Blessed are you when men reproach you, and say all manner of evil against you, for my sake. Rejoice and exult, because your reward is great in heaven; for so did they persecute the prophets who were before you" (Matthew 5:3–12).

Since it is obvious from everyday experience that the merciful do not always obtain mercy and that those who mourn are not always comforted, then we must conclude that, if the Bible is correct, these promises must be fulfilled in a life "hereafter." While many are skeptical of this possibility, nevertheless, it can now be shown by a process of reason that, indeed, such is the case. But before we investigate the logic of a nonmysterious hereafter, let us first analyze the justification of God's laws as they pertain to life here on earth, and we shall then see how the wisdom of God determined from the beginning that any and all men profit from obedience to these laws.

The time has come when man must understand that his conduct in society affects society in such a way that he, as an individual, is inextricably implicated in the consequences of that conduct: the skyjacker who comes away from his adventure with a bundle of money may feel that he has profited from the deed; but in reality, he has not. For the mechanics of such behavior create a less pleasant world for him to live in.

A child who secretly gorges himself on candy may feel that he is having a good time, but we know that the child may suffer rather immediate consequences in the form of an upset stomach, or he may suffer in the future from a deterioration of his teeth, or he may suffer from diabetes. In any case, it will be difficult for the child to perceive that the pleasantness of the candy could be anything but gratifying.

And so it is with those who violate God's laws: The pleasures of the moment may delude them into believing that they have profited by their experience, but true happiness will elude them in proportion to their violations—and the sad part is, they will never know the difference.

Because man is a social animal, his happiness depends upon the society of which he is a part. And, being a part of that society, he also governs, to a large extent, the happiness of others. It does not require a mental giant to perceive then that a happy society is conducive to the happiness of its members.

Peace of mind is perhaps the greatest asset to happiness that any individual may have. If we can allow our daughters and other loved ones to move about in our city streets without fearing for their safety, then we in turn will act in a manner to make our society a place where others can find ever greater happiness.

Consider as an example: Would you rather live with a happy family (a small-scale society) who obeyed the laws of God, or would you rather be part of a family where dishonesty, violence, and sexual perversion were practiced? Perhaps there are those who would agree that dishonesty and violence are bad but who can't see anything wrong with sexual perversion. In fact, there are many (even among the clergy) who find the Bible's preoccupation with sexual morality irrelevant or picayune. These are the members of society who say it is nobody's business what two consenting adults do in private. They assume that the Bible either is fradulent (not the Word of God) or that they are wiser than their creator. In either case, they are wrong because the practitioner of sexual perversion inescapably injures his psyche (mental life).

The pervert may or may not be aware of the injury he does himself; but, nevertheless, society will suffer insofar as the pervert does not function at the peak of his capacity. (A ballplayer who does not stay in shape hurts not only himself but also the entire team.)

The Lord God, in His great wisdom, created living creatures with the basic appetites to insure their survival, and He made the satisfaction of those appetites among the most pleasant in life. But He recognized that the satisfaction of the appetite for sex could be attained unnaturally and thus lead to character deformation. For that reason, at the outset, He admonished Adam and Eve to refrain from the unnatural satisfaction of the sexual appetite. Eve, however, foundered, and man came into possession of the knowledge of evil sexual gratification; and, since he was already aware of the good and natural gratification of the sex drive, God said of him: "Indeed! the man has become like one of us [members of God's society] knowing good and evil" (Genesis 3:22). This is not to suggest that God's society practices unnatural sex, but merely that they know of it.

Recognizing man's frailties, and being aware of his sensitivity to his environment (the rest of society), God tried to build into man that strength of character which can only come from practicing restraint. God knows that, to a large extent, we act as we see others act. But the wise man will listen to God and practice restraint in all his appetites, and in so doing he will grow in self-respect, gaining inner strength and reflecting his goodness on the rest of society.

You see, your influence on society is like the field of a magnet: it is infinite, exerting a great force on those objects in close proximity and an ever-diminishing force on objects further away. And so, since you are part of society, so also is society a part of you.

This concept will, perhaps, become clearer if we view the community of man with the same perspective as does God. While it is obvious that God *does* have compassion and concern for each individual human being, it stands to reason that, with His great perspective, He views the whole of earth society as a single organism. (This same concept, man has often applied in studying societies of ants. Each ant in a colony, for example, has a specific function; so that viewed as a whole, the colony can be considered a single organism.)

Looking at man in the same perspective, we see that any malfunction of a member of society affects every other member. A society in which some members enjoy a surplus of commodities while others suffer deficiencies will not function healthfully. And a society whose members are not concerned with the well-being of the group, but rather with their own individual pleasure, will find that in the long run the greatest pleasure comes from being a member of a healthy society.

This same perspective can also be applied to a view of the human organism: the individual cells being counterparts of the members of a society. And the analogy here is surprisingly exact: in our bodies we have armies to protect us from invasion from foreign bodies; we have repairmen; we have waste-removal agents; we have messengers, etc.

But what happens if we don't take care of all these members of our body community? What happens when a few cells decide that the coronary orgasm produced by nicotine inhalation is pleasurable? Do all the members of the body community benefit from this orgy? Obviously not, for, in the end, all the society will suffer the consequences of this abusive act—including the cells who determined that the act was pleasurable.

If this entire concept were not so important and so obvious once grasped, I would not further belabor it; but for those who may still be a little hazy on the implications, allow me to offer one more thought on the subject. Since transgression on the rights of others can cause circumstances whereby those "others" (because of the transgression) will violate the rights of still others, we can recognize a domino effect which, in this case, is circular. For example, suppose every member of society were wired in series (one wire). And suppose the Golden Rule said, "Do not apply electric shock to your neighbor." Then we should quickly find out why this was a good and valid rule!

While we may not be wired to one another electrically, we are, nevertheless, just as vulnerable to the discomfort which our acts cause our neighbors. The circuit may not be completed as quickly as with the electric shock, but just as assuredly, it will be completed! If, however, we do not live long enough to suffer the consequences of our sins, then we will find that payment will be made in the hereafter.

The evidence for a hereafter, as recorded in the Scriptures, is monumental and conclusive; but the obvious problem involving a belief in life after death is that such a belief seems to insist on a belief in things supernatural. In the past, there seemed no alternative to this dilemma: one either believed the scriptural promise of a life after death which involved a supernatural soul or spirit, or one simply denied such superstitious nonsense. But now, with the dawn of reason, it can be shown that, indeed, life after death is technologically feasible; and the abhorrent stigma of subjecting oneself to a belief in the supernatural is not necessary.

No passages of Scripture which refer to the hereafter ever suggest that conditions in defiance of nature's laws are involved. Such a conclusion (as pointed out in reference to other accomplishments of God) has been the result of man's inability to perceive that his science, compared with God's, is primitive.

Before investigating the technology involved in the survival of death, let us first clearly understand what the Bible says about it. In Daniel 12:2, the prophet, in clear, concise terms, tells us that, at least for some, there will be an accounting, both for sinners and for those who have obeyed God's laws. He says, "Many of those who sleep in the dust of the earth shall awake: some unto life everlasting, and others unto reproach, to see it always."

And in Matthew 5:25 we read: "Come to terms with thy opponent quickly while thou art with him on the way; lest thy opponent deliver thee to the judge, and the judge to the officer and thou be cast into prison. Amen I say to thee, thou wilt not come out from it until thou has paid the last penny." Quite obviously, what is being said here is that we should do as Christ taught us in the Lord's Prayer: that we should "forgive those who trespass against us." For if we do not, and we cause others to anguish because of our spite, then we shall have to pay in the hereafter. Furthermore, we see that we shall have to pay in proportion to the anguish we cause.

However, it should be noted that a literal prison for the purpose of incarceration does not make sense, particularly in view of some other considerations which the Bible points out. Rather, I think it will become obvious, as the evidence mounts, that the prison of this passage is a figurative one.

In Genesis 9:6 we are told, "Whoever sheds the blood of man, by man shall his blood be shed." Now, as we are well aware, all murderers are not themselves murdered; so, if we are to believe this passage, we must admit that murderers are themselves murdered in the hereafter. And, indeed, we shall see that this can be done through technology.

Believers have never doubted the biblical admonition "Whatsoever a man sows, that shall he reap." But there is much confusion as to just how God intends to dole out His particular justice. Many believe that punishment for sins will be administered by Satan in a fiery hell, but this belief is not consistent with reason, nor is it in agreement with the text of the Bible.

Concerning the matter of reason, the belief that all sinners are cast into an eternal fire does not take into consideration the fact that all sinners are not equally evil. Justice can be served only by an equitable distribution of reward and punishment: the greatest sinners must receive the greater punishment, while those who have sinned less must receive less punishment.

The quote from Matthew 5:25, above, indicates that sins must be paid for in proportion to the sin: "thou wilt not come out from it until thou has paid the last penny." And so, we ask, what happens after payment of the last penny? Does it not appear that this passage does suggest that we shall be restored once payment is made?

We have already seen that God has promised that murderers must suffer by being murdered themselves. And to further strengthen the literal interpretation of that passage from Genesis, we see also in Wisdom*

* A Book from The Apocrypha.

11:17 the same promise: ". . . by what things a man sinneth by the same also he is tormented."

Once again, let me point out that not all of us are tormented by the sins we commit—at least not in this life. And so, once again, we are drawn inevitably to the conclusion that payment for sins is completed in the hereafter.

But must we pay for all sins? The Bible tells us that repentance will cleanse us of sin. In fact, God says, "I take delight, not in the death of the wicked one, but in that someone wicked turns back from his way . . ." (Ezekiel 33:11). From this, however, we should not hasten to the conclusion that sins are forgiven if we but turn away from wickedness. In our repentance it is absolutely essential that our sorrow for the sins we are repenting be at least as great as that caused to the victim of our sin. Nor does it do any good to feel vaguely sorry for having violated God's pronouncement against sinning. If one should violate the commandment against stealing, for example, forgiveness will come only when the thief suffers the anguish his thievery caused his victim. For, as will be shown, true repentance comes only with empathy for the victims of our transgressions.

While it is impossible to prove the existence of a technology in Heaven such as I am about to describe, it is nevertheless, as the reader must admit, a possibility far more palatable than the traditional version. Of course, for those who believe by faith or by the law, having been brought up from childhood accepting supernatural explanations of the conditions of Heaven, there is no need for a reasonable explanation; but, for those who simply cannot believe that man, in some mysterious, supernatural way, can be resurrected from the dead, brought to some exotic place called Heaven and there receive justice for his activities as flesh here on earth; for them, the explanation which follows will convince them that the possibility is well within the range of believability. And, of course, we have the irrefutable promise of Scripture: the conditions of a hereafter do exist. It is left to us then to determine only

the explanation of those conditions: Are they supernatural or are they technological?

In order to understand the process of resurrection, it
is necessary that we establish what it is that is to be
resurrected. To expect to be resurrected once again as
flesh does not make sense: Shall we be resurrected as
invalids if we died invalids? And isn't a fleshly body
residing in Heaven inconsistent with our concept of
Heaven? For example, what need would we have for
pain receptors in a place where the exclusion of pain
has been promised? And what of our digestive system?
Would it not be surprising to find ourselves harvesting
crops in Heaven? And, since there is no disease in
Heaven, we'd have no need of our immunological systems. In fact, we'd have no need of any of our fleshly
parts, for careful consideration makes it obvious that it
is not the body (any more than the clothing) which
makes the man, but rather, it is the thoughts, the emotions, the fears, the love, the pain, and indeed the entire
personality. And all of these things depend, in the final
analysis, on the memory.

Your father remains your father even though he may
lose an arm or a leg; and, should he receive a new heart
or liver or kidney, he remains your father. But should
he suffer a paralyzing stroke, robbing him of his
memory, and with it his ability to think, you will—
sentiment notwithstanding—tend to cling to the memory
of him before the illness. You will think of him much
the same as you would if he had died.

We are what we are primarily as a consequence of
what we have stored in the incredible memory units of
our brains. The human brain, according to recent
studies, has an unlimited storage capacity. Unlike the
static capacity of an electronic computer, the human
brain (in a manner not yet understood) appears to
have the capacity to enlarge (not physically) its storage
area as needed. The brain contains over a billion pro-
tein molecules which can change their electrical and
chemical structure. Conceivably, it is these changes in
structure which result in increased storage capacity.

Also, the electrochemical interaction of these molecules apparently forms new networks of memory storage.

We have the capacity to make cross-references within all areas of memory storage. Most of us view new information (whether visual, auditory, or tactile) in relation to information already on file, so that not only is the new information stored, but also the old information may undergo alterations.

Indeed, the brain is a marvelous device: some researchers claim that every sight, sound, or experience we have ever had is indelibly recorded in our memories. (Experiments with age regression under hypnosis tend to verify such a conclusion, for it has been found that subjects who have been regressed to earlier ages can remember such trivial matters as what they had for breakfast on a specific day.)

We don't begin to appreciate the complexity of the information-storing capacity of our brains until we begin to analyze the subject: we see not just a single object at a time, but literally millions of details in a glance at even the most mundane of objects. We hear sounds selectively, tuning in on one voice in a crowd when we so desire. By the sense of touch we distinguish between hot and cold, soft and hard, smooth and rough, light and heavy, sharp and blunt, etc. And the emotions we experience and record are unlimited.

But in all this, it is our sense receptors which carry the information to our brains. The eye converts light to electricity which is carried by the optic nerve to the brain where it stimulates the sensation of sight. (Direct electrical stimulation of this area of the brain has caused sightless persons to experience flashes of light.) The ear does the same with sound: The compressions of air caused by sound are converted by the inner ear to electric charges which are transmitted by the audio nerve to the area of the brain which interprets these impulses as sound. When we experience pain, the receptors transmit electric impulses along a network of neurons to record the sensation of pain in the brain, which, in turn, by an electronic message, instructs the

afflicted body part to withdraw from the source of discomfort.

It is because the information gathered by the brain
is first converted to electric impulses that we have good
reason to accept the promise of life after death. For, if
our brains can receive and record these electric impulses, then reasonably, the same impulses could be
received and recorded elsewhere. They could be received and recorded in a spaceship in the heavens
above us!

From Ecclesiasticus* 17 we read: "God created man
of the earth . . . and created in him the science of the
spirit. . . ." Notice, God did not put a mystical spirit in
man but rather He created in him a spirit based on
science.

How else could man be resurrected as promised over
and over again in Scripture if not by science and technology? In our primitive state on earth, we have succeeded in recording man's voice and with it, of course,
some of his thoughts. Is it not conceivable that one day
we shall be able to record emotions and memories?
Already, by implanting electrodes in the brains of
chimpanzees, we have found that pleasurable sensations
can be aroused by stimulating certain areas. And, since
experiments along these lines are in their infancy, may
we not assume that eventually we may stimulate not
only pleasure centers but also all other experience
centers, including vision, hearing, and pain?

The problem of how a sound recorded in our brain
by direct connection to the electric impulse carried by
the auditory nerve could also be recorded at the same
time by a device in the heavens (without a direct connection) may, at this time, seem excessively formidable.
But it is important that we remember that we are not
yet masters of nature. On the other hand, masters of
nature or not, we can see that this explanation makes
more sense than to say: God knows our thoughts supernaturally.

Experiments being conducted at Cornell University

---

* A Book from The Apocrypha.

indicate that it is possible to experience "sound" without the necessity of the electric impulses supplied to the brain by the auditory nerve. It has been found that subjects placed in a beam of electromagnetic radiation similar to radar experience a buzzing sound which, the subjects report, seems to emanate a few feet above their foreheads, and tests show that conventional hearing via the ear and auditory nerve is not involved. Rather, the sound-detecting area of the brain is being stimulated over a distance and with no direct connection!

And so, if sound can be beamed directly to the brain with no electrical connection, we have circumstantial evidence that possibly the opposite is true—that the electric impulses traveling along the auditory nerve can be detected and recorded over a distance with no connections. If this is the case, then we may assume that not only sound but all messages coming to the brain from our sense receptors may likewise be recorded in a distant device.

Thus we see, for the first time, a rational explanation of how God can hear our prayers and know our thoughts and how He can reward and punish us after death for our deeds as flesh. Obviously, however, God doesn't bestow justice on a recording device: the recording must be in a form whereby it is part of or all of an intelligent being. The most likely candidates for this position are the guardian angels as mentioned in chapter 2.

In Psalms 90:11, we read: "For to His angels He has given command about you, that they guard you in all your ways." And in Matthew 18:10, Jesus says, "See that you do not despise one of these little ones [children]; for I tell you, their angels in heaven always behold the face of my Father in heaven." Apparently, then, it is the guardian angels who record our lives, and it is only reasonable to conclude that they must know us intimately if they are to protect and guide us. "Do you not know that you are the temple of God and that the spirit of God dwells in you?" (I Corinthians 3:15). The protection the angels provide, however, cannot be physical: they do not snatch us from the path of a speeding train. Such interference is not allowed according to the rules outlined in Job 33:14, which reads:

"God speaketh once, and repeateth not the selfsame thing the second time. By a dream in a vision by night, when deep sleep falleth upon men, and they are sleeping in their beds then he openeth the ears of men, and teaching instructeth them in what they are to learn. That he may withdraw a man from the things he is doing, and may deliver him from pride. Rescuing his soul from corruption: and his life from passing to the sword. . . . If there shall be an angel speaking for him, [any man] one among thousands, to declare man's uprightness, he shall have mercy on him, and shall say: Deliver him, that he may not go down to corruption: I have found wherein I may be merciful to him. His flesh is consumed with punishments, let him return to the days of his youth. He shall pray to God, and he will be gracious to him: and he shall see his face with joy, and he will render to man his justice. He shall look upon men, and shall say: I have sinned, and indeed I have offended, and I have not received what I have deserved. He hath delivered his soul from going into destruction, that it may live and see the light. Behold, all these things God worketh three times within every one. That he may withdraw their souls from corruption, and enlighten them with the light of living."

Again in this passage we see that *God* and *angels* are interchangeable terms, for in the psalm it is the angels who guide us, while in Job it is God. The reason we find rules for angels is that (as pointed out earlier) man must have free will. The angels who speak to us at night while we sleep (via the telepather) are not allowed to repeat a message; for, just as a posthypnotic suggestion repeated over and over is strengthened, so also a direction from the telepather which is repeated will be strengthened; and, at some point, will even insure action. And once positive control of its subjects is established, God's society will have defeated its own purpose, which is: to live our lives with us and to experience the obstacles in life to which our society is subject. (Remember, God's society, as masters of nature, has no obstacles.) And the rule of "only three messages to each of us" was, obviously, instituted for the same reason.

It seems that there must be a certain skill involved in knowing when and what instructions they are to give. At any rate, we have been told many times over in Scripture what penalties and rewards the angels receive for their endeavors in our behalf. We have been told that "by what things a man sinneth, by the same also he is tormented." Keeping in mind the fact that an angel, living your life with you, is indeed you (he is recording your life just as you are recording it), we can see then that your death as flesh does not obliterate your memory units. For your angel lives on, carrying with him the personality that was (is) you, as well as the personalities of others in his charge before you.

It is important that we realize that our angels are really we; that if when we died another brain, charged with all our experiences, were to be transplanted into another functioning body, we still would live. And so also we will live on in the bodies (not flesh) of our angels. But since, as the Bible teaches, there will be an accounting in Heaven, it is obvious that the angels (as we) will be held accountable. However, payment will not be made until the "end time." The reason for such a delay (at least two thousand years) is that guardian angels take on new subjects upon the death of their present charges, and so they do not have time to pay penalties or collect rewards.

It appears that the timetable for the growth and maturation of earth's society falls into two-thousand-year cycles: we had two thousand years of law (childhood) and two thousand years of faith (puberty), and if the cycle continues linearly, we have two thousand years of reason (adulthood) remaining.

When the "end time" comes, however, there will be no new flesh over which the angels will have charge, and that time will be the time of judgment. Unless one prefers to think that it will happen supernaturally, we can offer a reasonable explanation of exactly how reward and punishment will be handled in those days.

To begin with, it should be pointed out that not all of us will be "raised from the dead." As the quote from Daniel says, "Many of those who sleep in the dust of the earth shall awake . . ." Not all, but "many." Those who will not arise will be the mentally incompetents and those who died as infants; they, obviously, have no debts to pay or rewards to collect. There is also the very strong possibility that those living apart from the mainstream of society, and thus being unfamiliar with the Word of God (as given in any of the great religions), will be excluded from judgment.

Often the Bible speaks of the "elect" without ever explaining the nature of the classification. But it would seem that the word pertains to those who have been elected to hear the Word of God. At any rate, we do know that there will be some who will not be held accountable.

If indeed it is possible that our lives can be recorded in a storage unit other than our brains—namely, in the storage unit of a heavenly being—then it should also be possible to store it in a third unit at the same time. To find that a perpetual system of memory tapes were being recorded and filed in a massive memory bank in Heaven would clarify our understanding of God's technology as it pertains to His method of distributing justice.

To punish us in the hereafter, God could have our angel tuned in, or set in the manner of a clock, to the time in our lives when we committed a sin. For example, if you had committed the sin of stealing, your angel (through whom you will again be you) will be subjected to the juxtaposition on his (your) consciousness of the tapes of those injured by your sin. And you will thus become the victim of your own crime! "By what things a man sinneth, by the same also he is tormented."

The debt for the sin of stealing, as well as the debt for all other sins, will not be repaid simply by experiencing the frustration, pain, and hardship of the victim of our sin; for sin is like an expanding water ring: its effects will cause unhappiness to others as well as to the immediate victim. Those who love the victim, seeing him suffer, also will experience some of the pain caused by the sin. And the rest of society, knowing that they could be the next victims, also will experience discomfort. Still others in society will be encouraged to follow the example of the sinner, thus causing even more suffering. And you, as the sinner, will have to suffer the agonies of a million victims and subvictims for the mere act of stealing perhaps a twenty-cent item from a department store. That is indeed a high price to pay; but then, society, remember, also was forced to pay a high price for your sin.

God did not make His laws simply because the words sounded good, but rather because He had the wisdom to see that much great pain is the consequence of sin.

On the other hand, much great joy is the consequence of obeying God's laws. In the days of judgment, therefore, not only will the sinners be punished, but also those who caused happiness by obeying the laws will be rewarded. They (their angels) will be allowed to tune in and live the happy moments that the "good" people caused.

And so, whether or not you believe in the existence in Heaven (spaceships in the sky) of the technology I have just described, you should realize that, for your own greatest chance for happiness, you should obey God's laws. For as pointed out earlier, you are only as happy as society will allow you to be . . . and you are part of that society.

We are now entering the age of reason; the days are upon us when we must understand that only the childish in heart and mind will continue to seek happiness outside the laws of the Creator. However, we must not conclude that because we are entering the age of adulthood we should forget the father image, Jesus. He is part of our heritage and, whether directly or indirectly, He will always rule our lives. (Look for verification of this fact sometime before the year 1980, when the contents of the secret message of Fatima will be revealed.)

CHAPTER 8
Today's Absolutes:
Tomorrow's Absurdities

The great Albert Einstein, whose work inspired the ideas I am about to present, once expressed the thought that the explanations of the physical world are truly simple. In one of his lectures he said: "Our experience hitherto justifies us in believing that nature is the realization of the simplest conceivable mathematical ideas." Yet, paradoxically it seems, the explanations of nature given by Einstein in his relativity theories seem complex.

Why is this so? Why do Einstein's laws of relativity, which offer a simpler, more inclusive view of nature than Newton's laws of motion, appear to be more complex? Actually, the answer to this question falls in the category of a general truth; that is: Knowledge which is acquired through sense experience always appears simpler than that which we acquire through deductive reasoning. It is because Einstein asks us to look beyond the range of our experiences in the quest for understanding that we find his ideas complex. On the other hand, Newton, in formulating his laws of motion, merely called our attention to observable phenomena.

It is because the ideas I am about to present fall in the category of deductive reasoning that the reader may feel they are complex. Unfortunately, however, the mechanics of mass and gravity are impossible to experience. By our senses alone we can only measure the effects of mass and gravity; we cannot see the causes. And so, if we are to understand these causes (which causes we are certain must exist), then we must resort to reason.

Understandably, then, the reader may find the following treatise somewhat complex; an explanation of the mechanisms of mass and gravity could hardly be less so at this point in the history of science. And the fact that this explanation will also reveal the process by which matter is created will not lessen the complexity.

At any rate, to those readers who understand the following material I can promise a fascinating intellectual experience, and to those who do not, I think you will, nevertheless, enjoy walking on the edge of discovery.

A wise man once said, "The more you know, the more you know you don't know." A beautiful proverb, but alas, it rarely is true. Particularly when one specializes in a field of study does he tend to accept his knowledge of the subject as infallible and often forgets that many of yesterday's absolutes are today's absurdities. Scientists, schooled in the dogma of Newtonian physics, were aghast and befuddled by Einstein's relativity theories. One might therefore expect that these same scientists would, as a consequence of having their absolutes shattered, assume a more flexible stance in their appraisal of the evidence of propulsion systems which appear to defy laws of physics. I refer, of course, to the propulsion systems of UFOs.

Throughout the history of science, mankind has been plagued by the egotistical insistence by men of "science" that, if they didn't know it all, then at least they knew almost all. This stereotype of men of science must be discarded in our new age of reason. The mature society must recognize the value of humility and never become confident that it knows it all. For the know-it-all phase of life comes with impetuous youth; and our society, while not yet mature, is, however, in a transitional stage. From this point onward in the story of mankind we shall see tremendous forward strides in all fields of science and in technology; and seldom shall we see again such irrational thinking as is now prevalent among many learned men of science. Never again shall we hear them say, "With my knowledge of physical science, I know it can't be done." Instead, they will confess that what they know may not be the whole apple, nor, for that matter, even the seed; but perhaps only a fragment of the skin.

My purpose in the following discourse is not to present a studious, mathematically oriented explanation of UFO technology; I am neither a mathematician nor a scientist. Rather, my purpose is to jolt world society out of its youthful impetuousness and perhaps, once and for all, teach it that any and all absolutes must be viewed with great caution. Not for another two thousand years will mankind become masters of nature; yet, throughout history, societies have always felt that what they didn't know was so little as to be inconsequential. Today's scientists are no different: "UFOs cannot (as a consequence of physical law) make ninety-degree turns while traveling at speeds in excess of a thousand miles an hour." Reports of such nonsense, they conclude, are untrue because they "know" that the law of momentum (mass times velocity) would create inertial forces on board such a craft which would crush not only the occupants but the spacecraft itself. Therefore, claim the learned men of science, all such reports (millions) are either lies or the results of mistaken identities. However, they never explain what particular phenomenon of nature makes it appear that speeding objects can make 90- and 180-degree turns without changing velocity.

The situation is analogous to that which some isolated tribe of people on a remote island might experience if suddenly air routes were to be established over their island. A steady stream of reports would start to build in which the sighters would describe what they saw: an object like a great bird with unmoving wings; and eyes which flashed red and green; and a voice which roared but which always seemed to trail the great bird.

The medicine men (scientists) on the island would claim that these reports were nonsense; that birds cannot fly without flapping their wings and that their eyes cannot be different colors. And they cannot have voices which trail them. In short, their explanation would be based upon their knowledge of physical science. (Which, in fact, they would consider to be nearly infallible.) This case is completely analogous to what we are facing today in the realm of UFOs.

What the medicine men don't realize, however, is that their knowledge of physical law and technology is fragmentary: they know only enough to explain certain aspects of known phenomena but not enough to explain all phenomena.

Getting back to the problems involved in trying to explain UFOs and their technology, we must first readjust our perspective. We must face the fact that earth society is somewhat primitive by universal standards. For example, it never occurs to us that, once we develop spacecraft capable of reaching the stars, we may find that we are not allowed to visit and make contact with any and all civilizations. As a matter of fact, the evidence seems to indicate that open contact between different worlds is taboo. Not a great deal of imagination is necessary to figure out why. For example, if we wish to study a culture which has been cut off from the mainstream of civilization, we don't first "civilize" that culture.

Evidence that restrictions prohibit contact between worlds is to be found both in the Bible and in the obvious illusiveness of UFOs. Incidentally, UFO illusiveness has long been viewed as circumstantial evidence that they do not exist. This, however, can be accounted for by the fact that we have a narrow perspective: our world is the planet Earth, and on planet Earth there are no restrictions on where we travel and with whom we make contact. As a result, we see no reason why there should be rules governing UFOs making contact with us.

The Bible speaks of errant angels and "Sons of God" who came to earth and mated with the "daughters of men." From this we can deduce that some of God's "mature" societies did not obey the laws pertaining to open contact; and, as the Bible says, they were punished.

It would seem, therefore, that the society here on earth will one day become capable of intergalactic travel, as apparently have others of God's society, and that we too will have to obey certain restrictions. (I believe that any society in the universe which survives to maturity will be knowingly subject to God's laws and will thus be known as "Sons of God." This includes the society on earth.)

In attempting to show how contemporary men of science suffer an acute case of dogmatism, I will show how, indeed, UFOs defy no laws of physics but merely utilize laws which are as yet unknown to mankind.

Looking once more at the formula for determining momentum, we see that the law states that momentum is that force which accrues as a result of inertia. That is to say, an object in motion tends to stay in motion. Two factors determine the value of this force: One is the velocity of the object, and the other is its mass. Thus, the formula reads, $M=mv$. Where (M) is the momentum, (m) is the mass and (v) the velocity. It should also be noted that momentum is a vector quantity; the direction being that of the motion of the body. From this formula we see a clue as to how UFOs appear to experience no inertial effects. For if the value of (m) mass could somehow be made zero or nearly zero, then there would be little or no momentum. Zero times any number is zero.

Newtonian physics, and for that matter, relativity physics, makes no attempt to explain gravity or mass, but instead only describes their effects. It is precisely for this reason that physicists cannot conceive of an object having zero mass and thus cannot conceive of an object being unaffected by inertial forces.

An explanation of the nature of gravity and mass may at first seem complicated; but if the reader will refer to the accompanying diagrams, I believe that it will become clear that all is indeed simple—so simple, in fact, that it is illusive.

Let me start by reviewing the definition of the three

states of matter. Any elementary science textbook states it thusly: Matter exists in three states: gas, liquid, and solid. The considerations which I shall present will show a correlative view of the states of matter and the states of space. I am proposing that space exists in the following three states: undistorted, partially distorted, and completely distorted. Later, it will become clear what is meant by this definition, but for now it is presented only as background for what is to come.

Undistorted space is space wherein there are no gravitational fields. It is, in the truest sense, *nothing*. Partially distorted space is that space found in the vicinity of matter and is a byproduct of the creation of the matter: it is recognizable as the gravitational field, and in special cases exhibits itself as magnetic fields. And finally, completely distorted space is matter itself.

Philosophically and reasonably I think we could show that empty space precedes matter (matter needs space in which to exist, and we might therefore postulate that matter is composed of space; but a more expedient corroboration of this thesis is to be found in God's Word as given in Hebrews 11:3, where it says, ". . . and those things visible were made out of things invisible").

Empty space, and for that matter, partially distorted space, *is* invisible, but the effects of partially distorted space are very visible indeed. Perhaps there is no one who has never been fascinated by the performance of magnets. We hold them in one position and experience a force pulling them toward one another; turn one of them and a force now repels. Yet, with all this, there is nothing connecting them (or so it seems).

Even in a vacuum, magnetic fields are present; so also are gravitational fields; but the gravitational attraction between two objects is so slight that it is rarely of any consequence. The gravitational field of the earth, however, is a force which actually governs our existence but because it is forever with us, we are not fascinated by it as we are by magnetism; but, nevertheless, when one thinks about it, it is a truly remarkable phenomenon. For the space between the earth and a dropped object must have a character distinct from space where there are no massive objects like the earth.

So, what is the nature of this invisible space which science refers to as "gravitational fields" and which I refer to as "partially distorted space"?

To understand what I am proposing, the reader must first understand one of the basic postulates of relativity physics: *Absolute motion is nonexistent.* For example, if we should find ourselves in a windowless vehicle, there would be no possible experiment we could perform to establish whether we were in motion. In fact, the question of whether we were moving is meaningless unless we also define what object we are moving toward or away from.

Ordinarily, we use the earth as a reference point when we speak of our motion; but what do we mean if we say we walk three miles per hour in a southerly direction on a jet plane traveling four hundred miles per hour in a northerly direction? With reference to the plane we are walking three miles per hour toward the tail; but, with reference to the earth, we are traveling three hundred and ninety-seven miles per hour in a northerly direction. (Note: These figures don't take into consideration the earth's revolution or rotation, nor do they take into consideration the motion of our galaxy.)

Now consider the following thought experiment: Suppose, in an empty universe, you were to find yourself on board one of the only two spacecraft in the world; and watching through your window, you saw the second spacecraft drawing nearer and nearer. How would you determine which craft was moving? Obviously, there would be no way to resolve this problem. The best we can do is arbitrarily pick one of the objects and designate it as stationary. Then we can say that the other object is in motion. This means, of course, that it is equally correct to designate the other object as stationary. And so we see that the state of motion of an object is a designation rather than a condition.

We are confronted by the same problem when we try to determine size; there is no way to determine it without comparing it with something else. But because we are accustomed to this procedure of comparison when determining size, we are not surprised to learn that size is also a designation and not a condition.

Before Einstein, classical physics postulated an invisible substance called "ether," which was thought to permeate the cosmos. Thus, an object in motion was said to have absolute motion, meaning that it was moving through the stationary ether. However, through experiments involving the speed of light as measured while traveling against and with the "ether," it was found that the ether didn't exist, and so the theory was abandoned, and with it Newton's mechanical view of the laws of motion lost much of its appeal. Actually, however, the dilemma of the luminiferous ether, as it is sometimes called, has never been brought to a satisfactory conclusion. For one thing, we need the ether in order to explain the propagation of light; for, since light travels as a transverse wave (which type of wave manifests itself only in a material body), we must ask: What is the nature of this material body? Einstein himself summed it up as follows: "Space is endowed with physical qualities; in this sense, therefore, an ether exists. But this ether must not be thought of as endowed with the properties characteristic of ponderable media, as composed of particles, the motion of which can be followed; nor may the concept of motion be applied to it."

It will be shown that Einstein's description of space is quite accurate. Indeed, space *is* endowed with physical qualities. For when space is distorted in the manner I shall describe, the process is analogous to the whipping of cream. the liquid cream, while distinctly different in physical properties from the final solid, is, nevertheless, in many respects similar to the original liquid. So also is empty, undistorted space similar to the final product of distortion—matter.

With the discovery that motion was relativistic came also the discovery that time, length, and mass were likewise subject to variations which were dependent on a frame of reference. The one remaining absolute, according to Einstein, was the speed of light. (It should be noted that light is but a small segment of the electro-magnetic spectrum and that, no matter what the wave-length, whether it be radio waves, light waves, or ultra-violet waves, they all travel at the same speed.)

Einstein introduced some interesting thought experi-ments to show how time and distance are relativistic concepts. Perhaps the most famous of these concerns a man standing beside a railroad track who observes twin bolts of lightning striking "simultaneously" at equal distances up and down the track. At the same time, a speeding train moved along the track. Now, an observer inside the train, being exactly opposite the observer outside when the lightning struck, will also conclude that the lightning bolts struck simultaneously even though he will see the flash from the bolt in the front before he sees the flash from the rear. By adding his velocity to the speed of light he will see how the light from the forward bolt reached his eyes before the light from the rearward flash. And so, by doing his arithme-tic, he will conclude that both flashes occurred at the same time.

But keeping in mind that motion is relative, we can choose the observer outside the train as the one who is in motion (not relative to the earth but relative to the train) and the observer inside the train as the one who is stationary. We see immediately what this does to our concept of time and distance: If the observer in the train is stationary, then he does not need to add veloci-ties. He knows that the flash in the front of the train occurred first because he saw it first. But note: If this observer were forced to accept as fact the simultaneity of the flashes, then his only alternative would be to conclude that he must have been closer to the forward flash. But then he must explain what happened to the length of the train.

Another thought experiment which demonstrates the futility of trying to determine "true" length or time is as follows: An experimenter inside an enclosure made of one-way glass drops a rubber ball to the floor. He notes that the ball drops three feet and rebounds two feet; a total of five feet. He also notes that the ball drops straight down and bounces back up along the line of descent. And also, he notes the time the ball was in motion and computes its average velocity.

Now consider what would happen if an observer in relative uniform motion were to watch these proceedings from outside the glass enclosure. He would see the ball drop not in a straight line but in a curve, and he would see the rebound also as a curve, so the journey of the ball would appear as the letter *u*. And thus it would have traveled a greater distance than the enclosed experimenter had calculated, and hence at a greater average velocity.

The important thing to remember in both these experiments is that there are no absolute right or wrong measurements or assumptions. What is right for one frame of reference is actually right even though (seen from a different frame of reference) the answers are different. There is simply no escape from the reality: length, time, and mass are relative! (For those readers interested in further pursuit of these intriguing concepts of relativity theory, I have included a recommended reading list of nontechnical books.)

Without going into the details, let me state some further conclusions of the relativity theory, some of which have been verified by experiment. The theory claims that, to an observer at rest relative to a speeding object, the object will measure a shorter length than it would to an observer moving with the object. And, in fact, were it possible to attain the speed of light, the object's length relative to the stationary observer would be zero.

Also, it is claimed that any periodic motion (such as that of a clock) would measure slower to the observer whose frame of reference was stationary relative to the speeding object. But most important of all in our study of UFO behavior is the fact that mass would measure as greater from the point of view of the outside observer. And, if the object could attain the speed of light, the outside observer would measure its mass as infinite.

Such are the conclusions of relativity theory. It is significant to note that recent experiments with atomic particles indicate that mass does indeed increase according to the relativity formula when the particles are accelerated to speeds in the vicinity of 186,000 miles per second (the speed of light).

The formula for calculating the length of a "moving object" (remember, the object is moving only in relation to another object arbitrarily designated as stationary) is as follows:

$$(1) \qquad L_R \sqrt{1 - \frac{v^2}{c^2}} = L_m.$$

Where (L_R) is the length of the object when measured at "rest," (v) is the object's relative velocity, (c) the velocity of light, and (L_m) is the length of the object as measured from the frame of reference of an object in relative motion. The relativistic mass of an object varies inversely with the length so that the formula would be written thusly:

$$(2) \qquad \frac{M_R}{\sqrt{1 - \frac{v^2}{c^2}}} = M_m.$$

Where (M_R) is the mass of object when measured at "rest," (v) the object's relative velocity, (c) the velocity of light, (M_m) is the mass of the object as measured from the reference of an object in relative motion.

We see from both these formulas that velocities in the realm of human experience have little effect on mass and length, but that when the velocity approaches the speed of light, the effect becomes very significant. In fact, were the velocity to become equal to the speed of light, we see that in formula one, the value for length becomes zero and in formula two, the value for mass becomes infinite.

Accepting the fact that length is a relativistic quantity, we can now pursue a thought experiment which will explain both how empty space can become distorted, forming gravitational fields, and how ultimate distortion results in the formation of matter. Suppose that somewhere in a remote region of the universe where there existed no gravitational fields, we could arrange to provide an infinitely large ring of light—we could even think of it as a neon tube except it is better to imagine it as nonmatter. Theoretically, we could think of the circumference of this ring (since it is infinitely long) as being a straight line. Now, if this ring should be rotated faster and faster until it was moving at the speed of light, consider what an observer opposite its center would see.

When the speed of the circumference becomes a significant fraction of the speed of light, it would, according to the contraction formula, become shorter, and thus the diameter of the ring would become smaller. As the speed continued to increase, our observer would see the ring closing in on the center until, eventually, he would see what appeared to be a stationary point of light surrounded by a halo of ever-diminishing luminosity. The brightest point would appear at the center because the light from the whole ring would be concentrated at this point (where the diameter of the original ring had "shrunk" to zero).

If the reader has successfully visualized the thought experiment to this point, he should have no trouble in taking a further step. Instead of a ring of light we could have taken only the smallest part of the circumference: we could have taken a single point of light. And then by accelerating it in a circular orbit, we would obtain the same results. Our observer opposite the center of rotation would see (when the spot was traveling at the speed of light) a central brilliant light surrounded by a halo which grew progressively dimmer as the distance from the center increased.* (Recognizing the relativity of motion, we note that it is equally valid to designate the spot of light as stationary and the observer to be in motion.)

In the case of a single spot of light, as opposed to the original ring, the configuration of the course of our

---

* Since it is known that the strength of gravitational fields varies inversely with the square of the distance, one of the proofs of the proposals I am making here will be mathematical verification of the fact that the luminosity of the light in the above thought experiment diminishes in accordance with gravitational laws.

speeding spot would be an ever-diminishing spiral with the rings becoming increasingly dense as it approached zero diameter. Also, taking into consideration the relativity of time, we note that the time of each successively smaller spiral would also diminish until, at the center where the speed of light would be attained, time would stop. Then one or a billion or a trillion revolutions (which at the center would be rotations rather than revolutions) would occur in zero time. However, revolutions outside the center of the spirals would occur with progressively greater lapses of time (moving away from the center), thus accounting for relativity's proposal that gravitational fields have a slowing effect on time.

When it is remembered that nothing has happened to the spot of light, but that the space it occupies has changed, we then have a clue as to the nature of matter and attendant gravitational fields: elementary matter is the complete distortion of space found at the center of the spiral in our thought experiment, and the spiral itself, the intermediary between empty space and matter, is its gravitational field.

It is because we are physical, being composed of distorted space (centers of spirals) that our sense receptors have no capacity for recognizing characteristics of empty space, and thus we have no way to determine what it is that causes the distortions. Obviously, it is not a spot of light, as suggested in our thought experiment. But, nevertheless, space must have properties which allow the development of the distortions proposed here. If not, then we might have to conclude that gravity is a supernatural force. But since, as I will show, the distorted-space proposal will account for much that we now know about physical law and also explain much that we don't know, I feel certain that it will be accepted as true.

Actual physical matter, as perceived by our senses, must be composed of great numbers of these distortions. While I am not prepared to suggest the nature or name of the simplest particle, it *does* seem that an electron must be composed of many of these basic constituents, because an electron according to evidence established by the optical spectrograph, must be spinning or, in line with my reasoning, must be encased in a sphere of converging spirals. Possibly this effect results from a precession (rotation of the plane of the spiral), but I suspect that it results from the joining of a number of centers of spirals.

The attraction that particles have for one another can be accounted for by imagining what would happen when the arms of the spirals of two particles overlapped each other (see figure 2). Each experiencing the

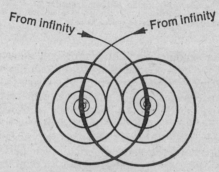

From infinity → ← From infinity

Figure 2: These two particles, experiencing a force (at points indicated by thickened lines) will be moved toward a common center. *Note*: These spirals are exaggerated for clarity. In all probability, they are much more dense.

inward motion of the other, would be brought to a common center. But this center, remember, would be impenetrable; it represents the complete condensation of space. When a sufficient number of particles accumulate, they manifest themselves as visible matter, of which all that we experience is composed.

A single atom would have, literally, billions of these spirals emanating just from the nucleus, and, I might venture, the orbits of electrons are somehow determined by the density of these spirals. At any rate, when enough atoms accumulate to produce visible matter, the number of spirals must be astronomical. The result is that we move about in a veritable maze of spirally distorted space. But, since the bulk of the earth's mass is under us, we experience only the effects of the upper portion of these spirals (see figure 3).

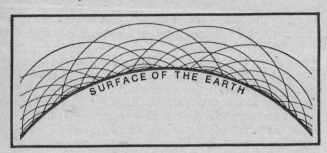

Figure 3: The centers of these spirals, being either at the surface or below, exert forces only toward the earth or parallel to its surface; but never away from it. (The spirals are distorted space. Refer to text.)

By use of another thought experiment, Einstein demonstrated the equivalence of uniformly accelerated motion and gravitational attraction. He suggested that a man in an elevator out in space where there were no gravitational fields would experience a force indistinguishable from gravity if the elevator were to be accelerated uniformly (at a constant rate of increase). The occupant of the elevator could even perform experiments such as dropping objects and noting their rate of descent (see figure 4).

If, for example, the elevator was accelerating at the rate of thirty-two feet per second per second, then an object dropped inside would accelerate at the same rate. (This is the rate of acceleration for objects falling on the earth.) And, indeed, concluded Einstein, there could be no way the experimenter could determine whether he was accelerating or was under the influence of a gravitational field. Generalizing this statement, Einstein said, "There is no experiment an observer can perform to prove whether or not he is moving, either in uniform or nonuniform motion."

Applying this concept to my proposal of the configuration of gravity fields, we see that it is equally valid to think of the space spiraling inward with resultant vector lines of accelerated motion toward its center, or to consider ourselves in motion in opposition to these resultant vectors (see figure 5). Since, from one point of

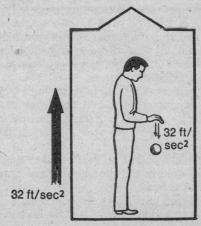

Figure 4: An experimenter in a uniformly accelerating elevator will not be able to determine whether he is in a gravitational field or whether he is in uniformly accelerated motion. Likewise, were he in a stationary elevator in a gravitational field, he would not be able to determine his condition.

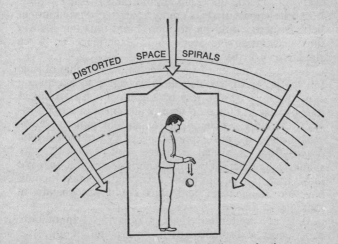

Figure 5: It is equally valid to choose the spiraling, accelerating space as stationary as it is to choose the man in the elevator. And thus we can say that he is accelerating uniformly.

view, these lines are accelerating uniformly past the observer, it is equally valid to choose the spirals as stationary and thus the observer will find himself in a position similar to that of the man in the elevator: he will find himself being uniformly accelerated and will experience gravitational forces.

Einstein also noted that, in a sufficiently long elevator, the experimenter would find that two objects dropped side by side would descend along parallel lines. However, in the same elevator at rest on the earth's surface, the two objects, under the influence of the earth's gravitational field, would converge as they descended— just as they would in the spirally distorted space of my proposal (see figure 6).

It can be seen then, that Einstein's reasoning does not refute my proposal, but I believe he has made an invalid assumption: he has assumed that inertial mass exists in empty space. He has assumed that Newton's law of inertia, *A body at rest will remain at rest and a body in motion will continue in motion with constant speed in a straight line as long as no unbalanced force acts on it*, is true under all circumstances. But I believe it can be shown that in empty space (no gravitational fields), there would be no inertia and thus our man in the accelerating elevator would experience no force similar to gravity.

Just as we matter-of-factly accept the fact that objects fall to the earth, so also have we come to accept the precepts of Newton's law of inertia. We say an object falls because it falls; and we say an object in motion remains in motion because it remains in motion. Obviously, these are not explanations; they are conclusions drawn from empirical evidence. But, seriously, why should an object in motion continue in motion? We know that if an object could exist with no mass it could have no momentum and thus could not remain in motion.

It is my contention that an object, set in motion, experiences a displacement of its gravitation spirals in such a manner that the gravitational spirals of the earth maintain the velocity of the object. The greater the

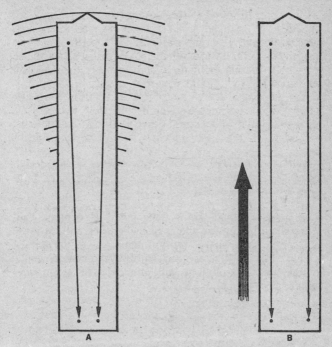

Figure 6: In long elevator A, under influence of distorted space spirals, objects will drop in a converging trajectory. In elevator B, accelerating upward, objects will drop in a parellel trajectory.

velocity imparted to the object, the greater the displacement of its spirals, and thus the greater velocity is maintained (see figure 7).

Since the idea that spirally distorted space is responsible for the phenomenon of gravity represents a new frontier in science, it will be necessary to proceed cautiously with theories related to the concept. For example, when I propose that gravitational spirals can be displaced by motion, I am making an assumption based on a reasonable possibility, but there is no way at present to determine precisely the characteristics of space distorted by the speed of light. The reasonable assumption, however, is that since the spirals originate

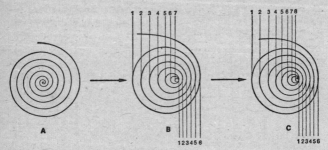

Figure 7: Particle A at rest has same number of spirals on left and right. Particle B moving from left to right has more spirals on left than on right. Particle C moving from left to right at greater velocity than B has more spirals on left than does B.

at a great distance from their eventual centers, the centers can be moved ahead of the spirals; and, as long as the object remains in motion, the shape of the spiral, at right angles to the motion, will become conical; and, in line with the motion, will present itself as an off-center spiral (see figure 8).

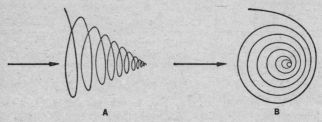

Figure 8: Particle A moving at 90° to the plane of spiral forms a conical distortion. Particle B moving in the direction of the plane of the spiral forms an off-center spiral.

If, as stated earlier, the vicinity of the earth is a maze of these spirals, then obviously the resultant forces parallel to the earth's surface must be in equilibrium—that is, the spirals must exert equal forces in all directions.

If we consider what happens to an object in the earth's maze when that object is in motion, we can see why the earth's gravitation maintains the object's velocity. For, if the motion of the object displaces its spirals, then there will be more spirals behind the object than in front of it, and thus there will be more spirals against which the earth's maze can exert a force; likewise, there will be fewer spirals against which the earth's maze can exert a force in the opposite direction (see figure 9).

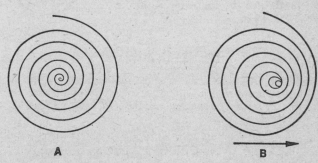

A   **B**

Figure 9: Particle A, at rest, has equal number of spirals on all sides. Particle B, in motion from left to right, has spirals displaced such that there are more on left than on right. Thus the gravity spirals of the earth, exerting force on all particle spirals, maintains the particle's velocity. *Note:* This concept does not conflict with the notion of the relativity of motion, for if we designate particle B as stationary and the experimenter as being in motion from right to left, the experimenter, while on the right of the particle will be moving in the same direction as the converging spiral, and thus see fewer spirals in a given time than he will see on the left side of the particle, where he will be traveling in opposition to the direction of the spirals.

To utilize this phenomenon and free an object from the gravity spirals of the earth, it will be necessary to distort the spirals of the object not only in one direction but in all directions. A start along this line of reasoning has been made by two physicists who are making a serious study of gravity with an eye to utilizing anti-gravity as a means of propulsion. A complete presentation of one their studies appears in the appendix and is included merely to demonstrate that the idea of anti-gravity propulsion is no longer a science-fiction dream but, rather, a subject worthy of serious scientific analysis.

Without commenting on the philosophy or conclusions of these scientists, I want to stress the important point of their experiment: Rotation somehow affects the inertia of an object!

While, to my knowledge, no one is experimenting with spinning static electric charges, I feel that ultimately this will be done; and when it is, I feel certain that we will discover the secret of the propulsion system of UFOs. Make no mistake, antigravity is a fact of existence. See the following from the Associated Press, Nov. 10, 1974:

SCIENTIST INVENTING ANTIGRAVITY
MOTOR SPACESHIP

London (AP) A British scientist said Saturday; he is on the threshold of inventing an antigravity motor that could fly a manned spaceship to the stars using nuclear fuel the size of a pea.

Eric Laithwaite, professor of heavy electrical engineering at London's Imperial College of Science and Technology, said the motor is based on the gryoscope, a rapidly spinning top that defies gravity. Gyroscopes already are used to guide spaceships.

"The motor is not easy to explain. If it was, others would have tried to produce one by now," said Laithwaite, who described himself as an astroengineer.

Laithwaite began working on the motor about six months ago after Edwin Rickman, who works with an electrical engineering firm, came to him with the idea. Rickman had patented it after he said it came to him in recurring dreams. Laithwaite incorporated in the device the ideas of another amateur inventor, Alex Jones.

Although Laithwaite is far from the production stage with his motor to defy gravity, the 53-year-old professor demonstrated its principle Friday at the Royal Institute in London.

Inside a box he brought before his distinguished audience were two electrically driven gyroscopes, each placed on a hinged metal arm fixed to a central pivot. Laithwaite made the gyroscopes rotate at high speed, and they rose into the air on the arms until they reached a curved rail that pushed them down again. The process then repeated itself again.

With the two gyroscopes motionless, the box

weighed twenty pounds on an ordinary kitchen scale. With the gyroscopes in motion, the contraption weighed fifteen pounds. Laithwalte said the loss of weight corresponded to the gravity loss produced by the spinning gyroscopes.

One major United States aircraft company is also working (secretly) on an antigravity propulsion system, and, I have been told, a partially successful prototype has been constructed. But I wonder if they and others in the field realize what is happening? I suspect not; I suspect that they are using and manipulating nature's forces by trial and error, not knowing why a system works but only that it does work.

Now, however, we can offer these scientists an explanation as to why certain experiments make it appear that an object can defy gravity. Now we can explain to them that all matter is formed by a spiraling distortion of empty space and that gravitational fields exist as a consequence of the creation of matter. The same force which directs the spiral toward its own center (remember, this force results from the fact that measurements of length decrease with increasing velocity) also directs neighboring spirals toward its center. This is gravity. On the surface of the earth all spirals closing in on the matter of the earth direct objects toward the earth's center, where the vector sum of the spirals is concentrated.

When experimenters spin an object—whether they know it or not—they are displacing some of the object's spirals in such a manner that the spirals of the earth cannot interact with them, and thus the object does not behave in accordance with the classical laws of inertia.

Also we might suggest to astrophysicists that they should consider the possibility that stars on the periphery of spiral galaxies are older than stars at the center of the galaxy. The circumstantial evidence of the theory proposed here is that the spiral originated at the outer edge and thus stars in this area must be older. (Remember, according to the Bible, the sun was born before the stars in heaven. Incidentally, one might suspect that if biblical authors were not inspired by God they might accept as fact some of the commonly mistaken beliefs of their contemporaries. For example, while most of the world at the time believed the earth to be flat, Isaias the prophet wrote: "It is he that sitteth upon the globe of the earth . . ." Isaias 40:22.)

We are truly just around the corner from the age of reason: the earth is not flat; the earth is not the center of the universe; microscopic organisms can kill gigantic man. And, most important of all, *supernatural* is not an explanation of anything.

God has given us the "Law" and He has given us "Faith" through father images. His rulership in Heaven remains, but now he recognizes us as an adult society, and, in a manner of speaking, has set us free. Has He *brought us up* properly? Will we use our reason, recognizing that God is wiser than we? And will we seek happiness through the wisdom of God, or will we perish through the folly of men?

Despite the conclusions of many presentday students of the Bible, the "End Time" is not yet upon us, nor will anyone have any valid idea when that time might come. The Bible says, regarding the Second Coming of Christ: "He will come like a thief in the night." That is to say, his coming will be a complete surprise.

While it is true that many of us die before living as adults, it doesn't seem likely that God would go to all the trouble He apparently has just to "bring up" a society and then allow it to perish before it has had a chance to exist through its adult phase. It seems much more probable that God has planned our existence on a time schedule which allows at least another two thousand years.

During these two thousand years, I am certain we'll experience a prolonged period of nonviolent existence. Emotions will play an ever-diminishing role in our decision making. In fact, I foresee the employment of a huge, impersonal, mechanical brain (a computer) programmed by the statesmen of every nation in the world to settle all disputes and to solve all problems.

Technology will solve the world food problems, the

pollution problems, and even the overpopulation problem. In the near future, theatrical entertainment will not
be audio-visual, but personal: the "viewers" will become the "actors," donning a headpiece which will
allow them to experience actual events through the
senses of another. (This device will be a primitive version of the instrument God's angels use to monitor us.)

Life expectancy will increase sharply with the medical advances soon to come. Artificial organs of all
descriptions will become commonplace in a few hundred years. Communication, both between individuals
and nations, will become so complete that not only will
we understand foreign ideas, but we'll even experience
the emotions underlying the birth of those ideas. And
transportation will be revolutionized by the employment
of antigravity propulsion systems.

But, best of all, most of us now living are going to
see the early signs of our mature society: Shortly we
shall discern a gradual but inexorable change. We shall
see a decline in the crime rate. We shall see nations
become disenchanted with the idea that might makes
right. We shall see a decline in the numbers of the
mentally disturbed. We shall see men become more
concerned with the well-being of society, and we shall
see a shift in society's mores concerning sexual conduct.
We shall see man once again living by the design of his
Creator and not flailing aimlessly in search of meaning
to his life.

And we shall see the beginning of the society envis-
aged by Christ where each man has empathy for his
neighbor. Thus will begin the age of reason.

"For at the resurrection . . . you will be as angels of
God in heaven" (Matthew 22:30).

APPENDIX

The Effect of Gravity on Rotating Objects

by Edward C. Delvers and Bruce E. DePalma

Summary: The predictions of a new conception of Reality have led the authors to believe that the inertial properties of real mechanical objects would be influenced by rotation. The results of a number of experiments concerning the interrelationship of inertia, rotation, and gravity are presented here; together with a theoretical discussion and analysis.

The Effect of Gravity on Rotating Objects

Introduction: An experiment has been performed in which the motion of a spinning object and an identical nonspinning object are directly compared in the presence of a gravitational field. Results of other experiments which have been performed (described in the report "The Force Machine Experiments") led to the expectation of a differential motion, and such a difference was actually observed.

Experiment: Two steel balls, 1 inch in diameter and each weighing $2\frac{1}{2}$ ounces, are pitched into trajectories which are recorded on film by stroboscopic photography. One ball rotates at 26,300 rpm, while the other serves as a nonrotating reference. The spinning ball is brought to speed with a 1 h.p. woodworking router motor (Sears Model No. 315–17370) and a variable transformer (0–140 volts). A cup which accepts the 1-inch ball is machined onto the motor shaft, with a conical inner wall at an angle of 25° to the shaft, making contact with the ball along a 1¾-inch-diameter circle. Attached to the motor housing is a similar cup in which is placed the nonrotating reference ball.

The experimental setup is presented in figure 1. Illumination is provided by a General Radio type 1531–A electronic stroboscope set at 3,600 flashes per minute (60 flashes per second). The resultant photographs are shown as figures 2a and 2b.

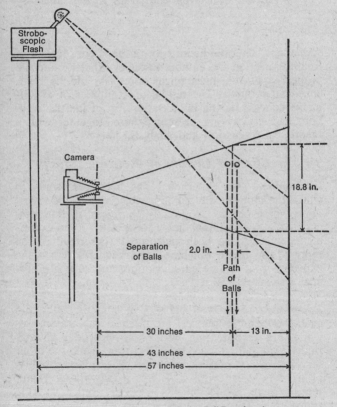

Experimental setup for the Spinning Ball Experiment

Figure 1

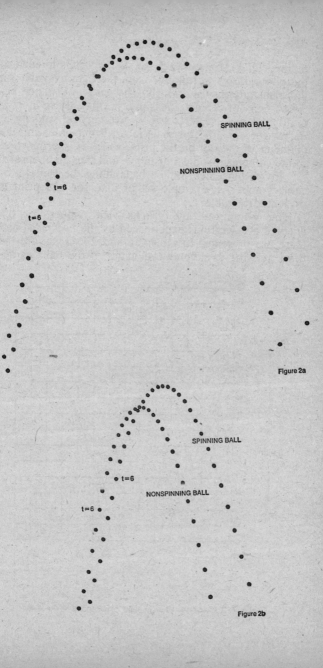

SPINNING BALL

NONSPINNING BALL

t=6

t=6

Figure 2a

SPINNING BALL

t=6

NONSPINNING BALL

t=6

Figure 2b

Velocity vs. time graphs for the two balls in each of
the photographs were made from the data available on
the print, graphs 1a and 1b. The vertical distance between two dot centers, measured in 60ths of an inch, is
multiplied by a scale factor to give vertical velocity in
inches per second. This scale factor is dependent on the
diameter of the dot on the print, which is in proportion
to the camera-to-subject distance, and thus compensates
for any displacement of the balls along the camera-to-
subject axis. An example set of data for one print is
presented in table 1.

The velocity-vs-time graphs yield values for the
average accelerations experienced by the two balls, and
these are presented in tables 2a and 2b. Given are the
times relating to different velocities of the balls as de-

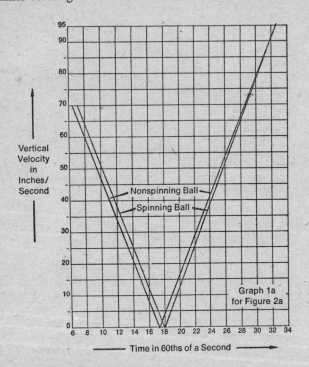

Graph 1a
for Figure 2a

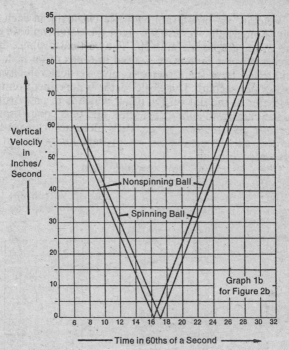

Graph 1b
for Figure 2b

Vertical Velocity in Inches/Second

Time in 60ths of a Second

termined from the graphs; average accelerations for the intervals between these points as calculated from

$$a = \frac{\Delta v}{\Delta t}$$

and the distances traversed in these intervals obtained from the equation

$$d = v_0 t + \tfrac{1}{2} a t^2$$

Distances read directly from the print (in 60ths of an inch multiplied by the scale factor) are given as a comparison to the calculated distances.

It appears that in its ascent the spinning ball decelerates at a lesser rate than the nonspinning ball and travels further, and in its descent accelerates at a

Table 1. Example set of data, for higher trajectory in figure 2a. Measurements taken from an enlargement of figure 2a.

exposure number* (t)	vertical distance in 60ths of an inch	diameter of dot in 60ths of an inch	scale factor	vertical velocity in inches per second
6		4.8		
7	32.3	4.7	2.240	72.4
8	29.7	4.7	2.236	66.4
9	27.0	4.6	2.232	60.3
10	24.3	4.5	2.224	54.1
11	21.6	4.5	2.220	48.0
12	19.0	4.4	2.216	42.1
13	16.2	4.3	2.208	35.8
14	13.2	4.2	2.200	29.1
15	10.2	4.1	2.192	22.4
16	7.3	4.1	2.188	16.0
17	4.5	4.0	2.184	9.8
18	1.6	4.0	2.180	3.5
19	1.6	3.9	2.176	3.5
20	4.6	3.8	2.168	9.9
21	7.6	3.8	2.164	16.4
22	10.8	3.7	2.160	23.3
23	14.0	3.6	2.152	30.1
24	17.1	3.5	2.142	36.6
25	20.3	3.3	2.130	43.2
26	23.5	3.1	2.116	49.7
27	26.7	3.0	2.104	56.2
28	29.8	2.9	2.096	62.4
29	32.9	2.8	2.088	68.7
30	36.1	2.5	2.072	74.8
31	39.6	2.3	2.052	81.2
32	43.0	2.2	2.040	87.7
33	46.4	2.1	2.032	94.4
34	50.0	2.0	2.024	101.2

* corresponding to time in 60ths of a second

greater rate than the nonspinning ball. Graphs 2a and 2b show the relationship of the calculated accelerations to each other and to the reference value 32.2 ft/sec^2, the standard value for gravitational acceleration.

Analysis: Judging from the results of previous experiments (performed with the force machine) the differ-

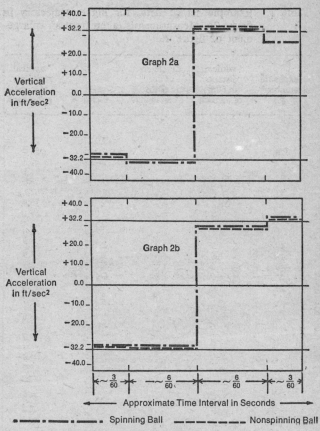

Graph 2a

Graph 2b

Vertical
Acceleration
in ft/sec²

Vertical
Acceleration
in ft/sec²

Approximate Time Interval in Seconds

Spinning Ball   Nonspinning Ball

Graphs 2a and 2b

ence in acceleration and deceleration between the spinning and nonspinning ball appears to be one arising from the condition of rotation of the ball. Certain limitations have thus far prevented the performance of the spinning-ball experiment in a vacuum, but the effects noticed are not solely due to any aerodynamic interaction.

Inaccuracies in the data-taking are not likely causes

Table 2a for data from figure 2a

		spinning	not spinning	value s / value ns	% change
vertical velocities and corresponding times, from v vs. t graph (graph 1a)	+ 60 ips, t_1	8.55	8.05		
	+ 40 ips, t_2	11.85	11.20		
	0 ips, t_3	18.00	17.35		
	− 40 ips, t_4	24.00	23.50		
	− 60 ips, t_5	27.10	26.85		
time intervals in 60ths of a second	$t_2 - t_1 = \Delta_1 t$	3.30	3.15	1.05	+ 5%
	$t_3 - t_2 = \Delta_2 t$	6.15	6.15	1.00	0%
	$t_4 - t_3 = \Delta_3 t$	6.00	6.15	.98	− 2%
	$t_5 - t_4 = \Delta_4 t$	3.10	3.35	.93	− 7%
accelerations as calculated from above data, ft/sec²	a_1	30.3	31.7	.96	− 4%
	a_2	32.5	32.5	1.00	0%
	a_3	33.3	32.5	1.02	+ 2%
	a_4	32.3	29.8	1.08	+ 8%
distances calculated from above data, in inches	d_1	2.75	2.62	1.05	+ 5%
	d_2	2.05	2.05	1.00	0%
	d_3	2.00	2.05	.98	− 2%
	d_4	2.58	2.79	.92	− 8%
distances measured from print, inches	d'_1	2.75	2.62	1.05	+ 5%
	d'_2	2.05	2.07	.99	− 1%
	d'_3	2.00	2.05	.98	− 2%
	d'_4	2.57	2.78	.92	− 8%
ratio a_2/a_3		.98	1.00		
ratio a_1/a_4		.94	1.06		

Table 2b for data from figure 2b

	spinning	not spinning	value s / value ns	% change
vertical velocities and corresponding times, from v vs. t graph (graph 1b)				
$+60$ ips, t_1	7.15	6.60		
$+40$ ips, t_2	10.45	9.85		
0 ips, t_3	17.05	16.25		
-40 ips, t_4	23.40	22.70		
-60 ips, t_5	26.45	25.80		
time intervals in 60ths of a second				
$t_2 - t_1 = {}_1t$	3.30	3.25	1.02	$+2\%$
$t_3 - t_2 = {}_2t$	6.60	6.40	1.03	$+3\%$
$t_4 - t_3 = {}_3t$	6.35	6.45	.98	-2%
$t_5 - t_4 = {}_4t$	3.05	3.10	.98	-2%
accelerations as calculated from above data, ft/sec²				
a_1	30.3	30.8	.98	-2%
a_2	30.3	31.2	.97	-3%
a_3	31.5	31.0	1.02	$+2\%$
a_4	32.8	32.3	1.02	$+2\%$
distances calculated from above data, in inches				
d_1	2.75	2.71	1.02	$+2\%$
d_2	2.20	2.13	1.03	$+3\%$
d_3	2.12	2.15	.99	-1%
d_4	2.54	2.58	.98	-2%
distances measured from print, inches				
d'_1	2.74	——		
d'_2	2.20	2.14	1.03	$+3\%$
d'_3	2.15	2.15	1.00	0%
d'_4	2.54	2.56	.99	-1%
ratio a_2/a_3	.96	1.01		
ratio a_1/a_4	.92	.95		

for the noticed differences, as seen by the close fit of the deceleration and acceleration of the nonspinning ball to the 32.2 ft/sec² reference, compared to the unsymmetrical yet consistent relationship of the spinning-ball behavior to the same reference.

The conclusion that can be drawn is that there is a difference between the nature of the interaction of gravity with a spinning object and its interaction with a nonspinning object. This observation is in line with the results expected of the experiment.

Gravity and the Spinning Ball Experiment
by Bruce E. DePalma

Introduction: The spinning-ball experiment consists of the observation of the interaction of gravitational and inertial forces on a rotating material object.

In the interaction of material forces on a rotating physical object, four experiments are possible:

1) Inertial forces acting on nonrotating material objects in field-free space.

2) Inertial forces acting on rotating material objects in field-free space.

3) Inertial forces acting on nonrotating material objects in a gravitational field.

4) Inertial forces acting on rotating material objects in a gravitational field.

Discussion of the Experiments: In experiments 1 and 3 we would expect the normal inertial forces summarized by Newton's laws of mechanical motion. In experiment 3, there is reason to believe there will be (supported by experimental evidence), a slight enhancement of inertia by the gravitational field. The cases of experiments 2 and 4 have not been adequately treated in the literature.

Behavior of Rotating Material Objects: Certain theoretical considerations justified the belief by the author that the mechanical properties of objects would be altered by rotation and that this would be the basis of the gravitational interaction. A series of experiments has been carried out supporting this basis of action. The report of some of these experiments has been appended to this theoretical dissertation. The results will be presented here.

1) Experimental evidence supports the fact that a rapidly rotating material object will gain in inertia.

2) The form of the gravitational interaction is that the additional inertia property, *od*, of rapidly rotating real material objects represents an additional repository for the extraction and supplying of work from or to a gravitational field. (This means a rotating mass will fall more rapidly [with greater acceleration] than a corresponding nonrotating object under the influence of a gravitational field.)

Form of the Gravitational Interaction: The complete description of physical phenomena depends on the result of many experiments. Together with the behavior of spinning-ball experiments, there is another series— force machine pendulum experiments—which have been reported elsewhere (c.f. reprints available). Basically, the phenomena reported here are summarized by these results:

1.) A force machine pendulum, i.e., a pendulum composed of two identical flywheels contra-rotating, for the cancellation of gyroscopic forces, swings with a period slightly increased over that of the nonenergized force machine. This indicates a net increase in the inertia of the rotating system.

2) The swinging of the energized pendulum is nonsinusoidal, with a foreshortening (flattening) of the peaks of the swings.

3) Mechanical energy of motion, stored in the created inertial property, *od*, appears as an *inertial field*. This inertial field has the property of conferring inertia on surrounding material objects; &,—a reduction in the frequency of oscillating electrical circuits placed in the vicinity of the energized machine.

When we examine the behavior of the spinning ball in relation to the above phenomena we can extract the following behavior:

When the spinning ball is thrown upward it leaves the cup with some vertical velocity v. In order to attain this velocity the spinning ball had been accelerated vertically prior to the time of leaving the cup. Acceleration of a rotating material object requires greater energy than a corresponding nonrotating one, since some energy is supplied to the *od* field. When the spinning object leaves the cup, the kinetic energy of motion is divided between the $\frac{1}{2}mv^2$ of the "real" mass of the object, and the energy stored in the created property, *od*. The sum of these two energies allows attainment of a greater height reached, in the doing of work against the gravitational field, in comparison to a nonspinning object moving with the same initial vertical velocity.

When we examine the behavior of the falling nonspinning object vs. the spinning object, we notice the spinning object falling faster (with greater acceleration).

We infer the behavior of the falling nonspinning object, falling in accord with Newton's laws, is a special case of the motion of objects in general. The more general case, involving rotation, is obscured by the gravitational interaction.

We would expect, if we could increase the inertia of an object (through rotation or by some other means), that the object would fall more slowly in a gravitational field. Let us consider, however, that while a conferred inertial property, *od*, would reduce the acceleration of a given body acted on by a given force *in outer space*; in the presence of a gravitational field, the conferred inertial property would be an additional mechanical "dimension" for the extraction of energy from the gravitational field in falling. Conversely, enough energy could be delivered from this "dimension" to cancel, or overcome, the mechanical energy extracted from an object raised in a gravitational field.

On this basis we may write:

for the spinning ball rising: $mgh = \frac{1}{2}m_o v^2 + K_{od}v$
for the spinning ball falling: $\frac{1}{2}m_r v^2 = \frac{1}{2}m_o v^2 + K_{od}v$

In a strict sense, the precise application of Newton's laws would have to be restricted to nonrotating mechanical objects in field-free space. In a gravitational field, the possibility of extraction of greater energy by a new mechanical dimension opens the possibility of an antigravitational interaction. In a rotating force machine, *od* energy can be supplied:

driven force machine: $mgh = \frac{1}{2}m_o v^2 + K_{od}\omega^2$

where ω is the angular velocity of the force machine drive axis.

Here is the possibility of the conversion of rotational energy to work done against the gravitational field. What is not determined at this point is the necessary increment of energy required to neutralize the weight of a given object, viz., it might take 1.1 foot pounds of work to lift a one-pound object one foot. The incremental field necessary to establish neutral weight or the hovering condition represents the inefficiency or lack of perfection of a real force machine. The important fact is the establishment of the *od* field as the mechanism for a mechanical interaction with the gravitational field *in addition to* the mechanical interaction expressed as Newton's laws of the falling nonspinning mechanical body.

Interpretation of Physical Laws: The fact that Newton's laws do not distinguish between the spinning and the nonrotating object represents the state of mechanical knowledge at the time. But because Newton did not distinguish between rotation and nonrotation, Einstein did not distinguish between the so-called inert and "gravitational mass." The fact that rotation affects the mechanical properties of objects places Newton's laws as a special case and invalidates a geometrical interpretation of space.

Many questions have been asked about the nature of

the gravitational-rotational interaction and its theoretical prediction. Basically, the theory can be looked at in the following way: If we consider a force—such as that engendered by the action of the gravitational field on a nonrotating real object—we find that we can make a measurement of that force on what we know as a scale. If we examine the reading on the scale, say one pound, we can conduct our examinations to that degree of accuracy where we can reach uncertainty. 1.0000000000????? It is not clear at that point whether the uncertainties in the measurement are due to properties of the experiment, or that which is being experimented upon. The levels of causes and effects, uncertainty. If we consider the results of any experiment we find this phenomenon.

If a real material object is rotated, it is found that within the body of the object are manifested the centripetal forces of rotation. If we consider a measurement of these forces we would find the same *defect*; that is, the measurment could be made precise enough to reach the noise level, i.e., causes and effects; and it would not be discernible whether the fluctuations were being caused by the experimenter or that which is being experimented upon. This level is the level of defect of forces and represents the connection between rotation and gravitation. Once there is established a connection, the transfer of energy follows a controllable orientation viz: The spinning ball falls more rapidly because such an object can extract more energy from a gravitational interaction than can a normal one, and as well, the storage of energy in a force machine as an *od* field, results in direct application of this energy to do work against the gravitational field and provide lifting force.

The concept of defect (of a field or force), was originally elicited epistemologically, forming the basis of the author's theory "Simularity," a theory of Reality based on the properties of measurement.

What are considered are the real properties of the level of causes and effects. What this represents physically is a form of inertia and a connection between rotation and gravitation. The "connectivity" of defect and the other real properties of inertia fields is better left to discussions to begin with the data presented herein. The theory is more properly left to the serious students of these ideas, as apprehension of the theory of Simularity necessarily entails the dropping of certain restrictions on the mind of the experimenter.

What can be said is this: In the further refinement of the art of physical conceptions, there are certain points reached wherein it is in the proper ordering of things to drop certain concepts when they have reached the end of their usefulness. In the search for the gravitational interaction, we have for long been hampered by the erroneous equation of inert and gravitational masses. We could better say: force is an element in the performance of two separate experiments; the force of gravitational attraction of a test mass; and the force necessitated to cause a test mass to accelerate at the same rate with which it falls.

Now that we have distinguished between the inert and gravitational mass by means of rotation, there are two principles involved:

1) The connection between all experiments through the mechanism of defect.
2) The resolution or distinction of experiments, one from another, on the basis of differing procedures. There is no basis to believe that two experiments involving a common element (ingredient) have any basis to be comparable in their results, viz., the particle-and-wave hypothesis of light. It is also reasonable to suggest that we not apply mundane concepts of "size," "weight," "mass," "spin," "sign," etc., without precise, explicit reference to the experiment being performed. Since many of the ideas we have about "matter" are conditioned by the models we construct, we may have reached a point of development where the "model" as a concept may have to be discarded.

It is not inconceivable to this author to regard physics as a collection of experiments, some of which may involve one or more common elements. No one experiment ever gives the results of another, separate and distinct experiment. Thusly stated: A different experiment gives a different result.

We can see that to take the common element of two distinct experiments, that is, to take force; and then take the *results* of the experiments, and then equate them. Having found them "equivalent," such a dilemma can resolve itself only in a curvature of a geometrical representation of space. In final analysis, the invariance of physical laws is replaced as a concept by defect, a real property elicited by the spinning-ball experiments, and which now replaces the invariance of physical laws as the unifying concept of all experiments.

17 March 1974

Simple Experimental Test for the Inertial Field of a Rotating Real Mechanical Object
by Bruce E. DePalma

Introduction: For the last five years, this investigator and others[1] have studied the mechanical properties of rotating objects for the purpose of application of certain heretofore undiscovered properties of rotation to new forms of propulsion machinery and machines with an antigravitational effect. The course of this investigator has not been to try to perfect new propulsion machinery, per se, but however to thoroughly investigate the phenomena of rotation.

The result of a great deal of experimentation, has resulted in a picture which relates the performance of certain non-conventional machinery (Dean, Laithwaite, Wolfe, DePalma) to a *variable inertia* property which can be engendered through motion of a rotating object.

In terms of the acceptance of a new body of information relating to the properties of rotating objects and variable inertia, a simple experiment has to be devised which clearly demonstrates the new phenomena. In the performance of experiments with large rotating flywheels, there are great experimental difficulties which result from experimenting on the large rotating flywheels themselves. Through a series of corroborating experiments it has been established that the anisotropic inertial properties of a rotating object are conferred on the space around the object. That is to say the space around a rotating object will have conferred upon it an

---

[1] Eric Laithwaite, John S. Wolfe, Edward Delvers.

inertial anisotropy. Let us ascribe this to the setting up of an *od* (odd) field through rotation of a real physical object. The purpose of the experiment to be described is the determination of one of the properties of an *od* field: the anisotropic inertia property.

The Experiment: A good way to detect a field whose effect is a spatial inertial anisotropy is to use a time measurement based on an inertial property of space and compare it to a remote reference. With reference to figure 1 we have a situation where the timekeeping rate of an Accutron tuning fork regulated wristwatch is compared to that of an ordinary electric clock with a synchronous sweep second hand.

The Accutron timepiece is specified to be accurate to one minute a month. Examination of the relative time drift of the Accutron-electric clock combination shows a cumulative drift of .25 second Accutron ahead for 4 hours of steady state operation. This is within the specification of the watch.

With the flywheel spinning at 7600 r.p.m. and run steadily for 1000 seconds (17 minutes), the Accutron loses .9 second relative to the electric clock.

Much experimentation has shown that the effect is greatest with the position of the tuning fork as shown. Magnetic effects from leakage fields from the gyro drive motors are almost entirely absent, any remaining leakage is removed by co-netic magnetic shielding. The Accutron is also in a "non-magnetic" envelope.

The purpose of the experiment is a simple demonstration of one of the effects of the *od* field of a rotating object. The demonstration may easily be repeated using any one of a variety of rotating objects, motor flywheels, old gyrocompasses, etc. The rotating mass of the flywheels used in these experiments is $29\frac{1}{2}$ pounds. The rotational speed of 7600 r.p.m. is easily accessible. The effect is roughly proportional to the radius and mass of the rotating object and to the square of the rotational speed.

Finer measurements can be made using an external electrically powered tuning fork oscillator and an elec-

tronic frequency counter. In this case, the inertial anisotropy of the *od* field of a rotating object can be much
more quickly and precisely measured. Field strength
lines can be plotted along contours of constant frequency shift for the two orientation conditions of fork
vibration direction parallel to, and perpendicular to, the
axis of rotation of the test object.

Conclusions and Observations: The proper conclusions
and evaluations of the above experiment will affect

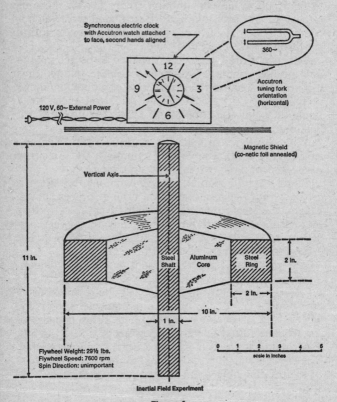

Figure 1

present conceptions of Cosmology. Before this can happen, simple tests must be performed to show the existence of a new phenomenon. It is hoped the apparatus for the performance of these tests is widely enough available to lead to quick verification.

Recommended Reading List

Blumrich, Josef F. *The Spaceships of Ezekiel.* New York: Bantam Books, Inc., 1974. London: Corgi Books, 1974.

Dione, R. L. *God Drives a Flying Saucer.* New York: Bantam Books, Inc., 1973. London: Corgi Books, 1973.

Durell, Clement V. *Readable Relativity.* London: G. Bell and Sons, Ltd., 1926. New York: Harper and Row, 1960.

Einstein, Albert. *Essays in Science.* New York: Philosophical Library, Inc., copyright 1934.

Gamow, George. *Gravity.* Garden City, L.I.: Doubleday and Co., Inc., 1962.

Gardner, Martin. *Relativity for the Millions.* New York: Macmillan, 1962. Pocket Books (paperback), 1965.

INDEX

Index

Aaron, assisting Moses, 57, 58
Abraham, 6, 9–10, 68
Angels, 14–15, 27–28, 30, 45,
    56, 61, 71–72, 79, 80,
    127
  aboard UFOs, 61–62, 65
  errant, 107–108
  guardian, 28, 29, 46, 99–
    100, 101, 102
  interchangeable with God,
    100
  as physical beings, 15, 16
Apostles, 70
Apostles, Acts of the, 78
Archaeology
  dating findings, 36–37
  substantiating Bible, 3, 35
Artificial insemination, 72
Atheists, 2
  and belief by reason, 18, 19
Augustine, Saint, 10

Babel, Tower of, 50
Balaam, 80
Baruch, Book of, 12–13, 67
Belief
  by faith, 18, 23, 47, 83, 85,
    95
  by law, 18, 23, 95
  by reason, 18
Bible, 1. *See also* individual
    books
  accuracy of, 3
  authenticity of, 11, 80
  on death, 93–94
  "elect" in, 102
  evidence of hereafter in, 93,
    94, 95

God dictated, 4, 12
God inspired, 4, 10, 11–12,
    125–126
  inaccuracies in, 12
  as key to salvation, 12
  miracles in, 26
  misinterpretations of, 2–3
  as mythology, 3, 44, 49
  omissions in, 41–42, 50
  preoccupation with sexual
    morality, 90
  purpose of, 12
  reasonableness of, 13
  teachings of, 2, 11, 19, 41–
    42, 95, 101, 107, 126
  technology in, 2
  truthfulness of, 77
Brain
  sense receptors of, 97–98,
    99
  storage capacity of, 96–97,
    98, 101, 102
Brain-manipulating device, 52,
    78, 84
Buddha
  and compulsion of faith, 9
  salvation through, 10
"Burning bush," 56

Carbon-14 dating process, 36–
    37, 45
Carthage, Council of, 10, 11
Cause-and-effect sequence, 5,
    14, 17, 72, 73, 74, 104
"Cloning," 48–49
Communicators, 79–80
Corinthians, Book of, 88, 99

PSYCHIC WORLD

Here are some of the leading books that delve into the world of the occult—that shed light on the powers of prophecy, of reincarnation and of foretelling the future.

- [ ] THE GOLD OF THE GODS
  by Erich Von Daniken   8477—$1.75
- [ ] THE DEVIL'S TRIANGLE
  by Richard Winer   8445—$1.50
- [ ] STRANGE WORLD by Frank Edwards   8045—$ .95
- [ ] PSYCHIC DISCOVERIES BEHIND THE IRON
  CURTAIN by Ostrander & Schroeder   7864—$1.50
- [ ] GOD DRIVES A FLYING SAUCER
  by Robert Dione   7733—$1.25
- [ ] NOT OF THIS WORLD by Peter Kolosimo 7696—$1.25
- [ ] WE ARE NOT THE FIRST
  by Andrew Tomas   7534—$1.25
- [ ] LINDA GOODMAN'S SUN SIGNS
  by Linda Goodman   6719—$1.50
- [ ] CHARIOTS OF THE GODS?
  by Erich Von Daniken   5753—$1.25
- [ ] MY LIFE AND PROPHECIES
  by Jeane Dixon   5547—$1.25
- [ ] BEYOND EARTH: MAN'S CONTACT WITH UFO'S
  by Ralph Blum   2564—$1.75
- [ ] EDGAR CAYCE: THE SLEEPING PROPHET
  by Jess Stearn   2546—$1.75
- [ ] THE OUTER SPACE CONNECTION
  by Alan Landsburg   2092—$1.75

Bantam Book Catalog

It lists over a thousand money-saving best-sellers originally priced from $3.75 to $15.00 —bestsellers that are yours now for as little as 50¢ to $2.95!

The catalog gives you a great opportunity to build your own private library at huge savings!

So don't delay any longer—send us your name and address and 25¢ (to help defray postage and handling costs).

BANTAM BOOKS, INC.
Dept. FC, 414 East Golf Road, Des Plaines, Ill. 60016

Mr./Mrs./Miss_____
               (please print)

Address_____

City_____State_____Zip_____

Do you know someone who enjoys books? Just give us their names and addresses and we'll send them a catalog too!

Mr./Mrs./Miss_____

Address_____

City_____State_____Zip_____

Mr./Mrs./Miss_____

Address_____

City_____State_____Zip_____

FC—9/75